The Tactical Walking Stick

A Practical System for using the Walking Cane/Stick as a Self-Defense Tool and Assistive Mobility Device.

Senior Master Len Lee
8th Grade Black Belt
Cacoy Cañete Doce Pares Eskrima
Doce Pares Fighting Art Systems

This work is dedicated to the memory of our Brother Sean Innes

Forward by GMAK

For me, Eskrima (a Filipino Martial Arts discipline) has been more of a lifetime journey of revelation and learning than a mere hobby. With many experiential happenings and adventures over the decades, I met with, trained, trained with, fought with, and befriended a large variety of people. Back at the turn of the century (that's not a phrase you get to use daily), an athletic, white-haired guy named Len Lee came into the gym, observed a single class, and begantraining as a constant student in my weekly Eskrima sessions. Len, being by nature a seeker and a searcher, was a natural fit for the training environment that comeswith practicing Eskrima; its diversity, practicality, usability, and functionality all appealed to and helped to reinforce the lessons he had learned in the 'Universityof Life'.

It's important to note that Len was a very accomplished individual before I ever met him, a husband and father, a Green Beret, an engineer, an engineering manager, and a practicing Martial Artist. Time, being a continuous flow, moving ever onward, has a habit of putting like-minded people together at the right timeand the right place to form a bond. So, it was perhaps inevitable, maybe only a matter of time before our paths crossed, and I was glad they did. Len soon became a 'core' enthusiast, attending as many training sessions, seminars, and camps as he could. On his own time, he began setting up training sessions with multiple classmates to get a chance to practice as much as possible. He soon began competing in Eskrima full-contact fighting competitions, and as he improved, he began winning, eventually going on to become a multi-time WorldChampion.

All senior students are given 'assignments' as they progress through the Black Belt ranks. This proves their mettle, allowing them to add some of their thoughts, innovations, and artistry to the fabric of our training system. Back before the COVID epidemic took hold of society, Len was due to be promoted once again. I assigned him the specific task of developing a thesis-level self-defense system focused on the humble walking stick (also known as the walking cane).

Eskrima, at its core is a 'stick fighting' art and lends itself easily to be the fundamental and conceptual basis for the development of a practical and effective walking stick Self-Defense System. The extended hiatus afforded to us by the worldwide pandemic meant that the assignment grew as I refined the objectives and parameters of what Len was aiming for. This was a huge benefit because rather than just ending up with an assignment coming from 6 months of R&D work (the usual time frame for an assignment), it came from 3 years of R&Dwork, revision, problem-solving, and innovation.

I am pleased to say that this book is the evolutionary distillation of that extended hiatus encompassing a practical self-defense system using the walking stick as a Self-Defense tool. Additionally, the introduction of basic fitness benefits, including neuromuscular maintenance development and basic physicalfitness utilizing the progressive exercises contained within the thesis, are beneficial to overall wellness. The system builds a beneficial relationship with thewalking stick for dealing with adversity in the ever-changing university of life andtimes.

This book is not the last word on this subject, but it is the first chapter in building a foundational relationship with the walking stick as an everyday tool toenhance safety, mobility, fitness, and quality of life.

I invite you to enjoy the read, begin the practice, and find your own truth.

Anthony Kleeman
Senior Grand Master
11th Grade Black Belt
Cacoy Cañete Doce Pares Eskrima
Doce Pares Fighting Art Systems

Preface by Len Lee

This book is the outgrowth of an assignment given to me by Sr GM Anthony Kleeman in March 2018. These assignments are given to senior-level students as a precursor to advancement within the Black Belt ranks of Cacoy Cañete Doce Pares Eskrima, Doce Pares Fighting Art Systems. My assigned task was to develop an effective Self Defense system utilizing the Walking Cane, also known as a Waking Stick.

Developing an effective Self Defense System of any type immediately struck me to be a monumental task. I definitely understood that a project of this scope would not be ready for presentation to a promotion review board within the normal six-month span. The COVID Pandemic and some personal medical issues expanded the timeline to over three and a half years. Working with GM Kleeman during this extended time frame, the task was expanded, updated, and clarified along the way to be more inclusive.

I began by researching material for the 'Street Smart' section of the project. I ended up spending a great deal more time than planned on the research as one finding led to another. I have observed and attended many Self Defense presentations/seminars which focused on how to fight off an attack while glossing over how to avoid being in the presence of someone who might do you harm to begin with. I found interesting studies regarding human predator behavior, including how they choose their targets and how to recognize them if approached. The studies and references are well worth the read for those interested in Self Defense.

To be an effective 'Self Defense' system, a solid foundation is essential. The bedrock of fundamentals of Cacoy Cañete Doce Pares Eskrima, Doce Pares Fighting Arts System was an easy choice. Early on, I enlisted my next-door neighbor who knows nothing about the Martial Arts other than what he views on television, to determine the ability of seniors to learn the foundational elements of striking and blocking. Additionally, I was fortunate to end up with a student who wanted to learn how to defend herself using a Walking Stick. She was instrumental in proofing the core striking and blocking exercises, role-playing exercises, and forms.

Many of the 'how to' books in my collection that employ photos were difficult for me to understand. The photos did not show intermediate steps making the flow of the techniques difficult to follow. Some simply have a ready stance photo with a final execution photo. The text description that went along with the photos often did not lead to further understanding. My goal was to get enough photos with supporting text in place for each technique or exercise to be clearly understood. After finalizing the book, I have found out just how difficult that can really be.

The section on using the Walking Cane as an assistive mobility device is not complete and will be updated with a Physical Therapy professional's input in a second edition.

Obviously, there is much content that can be added to this book. I have already started a list of clarifications and improvements. This edition provides a solid foundation for the system.

Len Lee
Senior Master
8th Grade Black Belt
Cacoy Cañete Doce Pares Eskrima
Doce Pares Fighting Art Systems

Table of Contents

Walking Stick/Cane Techniques for Self Defense

Introduction

Knowing how to defend yourself is highly desirable if confronted with the threat of violence. With violent criminal acts regularly reported on the evening news, many people (especially seniors) have become frightened to be out and about. For others, the belief that it "will not happen to me" is unfortunately pervasive and naive. In truth, violent acts are all too common, with many never even publicly reported. You never know if or when you may be targeted as a victim of assault. It could be a verbal confrontation that later leads to physical violence (a heated emotional argument), or one that starts with the intention to use physical violence as a means to an end (mugging, rape, carjacking, or a random act of violence).

So, what does one need to do to be able to defend oneself and their loved ones against violent situations? Most people immediately think of physical skills, such as punching and kicking in reference to self-defense. Know that keeping yourself and your loved ones safe from harm is more than learning how to punch or kick. The most important element of any 'Self Defense' system is avoiding troublesome/dangerous situations in the first place by becoming **"Street Smart"**. Practicing the principles of "Street Smart" will greatly reduce the odds of you becoming a victim, to begin with. If you unavoidably find yourself facing a physically violent situation, having the skill to efficiently defend yourself is key to your survivability and well-being.

If threatened with physical violence, having a Self Defense tool like the Walking Cane readily available helps to level the playing field. The Walking Cane/Stick system presented here targets the adult population and is particularly relevant to the Senior Citizen population (55 +). As with any physical activity, a minimum level of mobility and balance is required. Potential students should be evaluated to determine any physical limiting issues. The material is presented in a progressive manner, allowing the student to attain basic, intermediate, and advanced skill levels targeted to their individual physical capabilities and limitations. Once evaluated, confer with the student to baseline the targeted training level you believe they will be able to complete and what they should do to overcome physical limitations through additional training or Physical Therapy if applicable. Additionally, students must know that proficiency with this, or any other self-defense system requires commitment and continued practice.

While previous Martial arts experience is beneficial, it is not necessary. For those who have a background in the Filipino Martial Arts, the system is an addition to the basic skillset as we all grow older.

Becoming "Street Smart"

The most important element in any self-defense system is avoiding trouble. Learning to become **"Street Smart"** greatly reduces the likelihood of becoming a victim. When taking a neighborhood walk, answering your front door, or traversing the parking structure at the mall, being constantly alert and aware of your surroundings is key to not becoming a victim. The following discussion delineates actions and techniques to avoid trouble that should always be in the forefront of our minds.

It is Better to Avoid than to Run

It is Better to Run than to De-escalate

It is Better to De-escalate than to Fight

It is Better to Fight than to Die

Avoidance, Awareness, Vigilance, Body Language, and Intuition

Avoidance

Avoidance is the action of keeping away from or not doing something. Avoiding neighborhoods or areas that pose an overall threat is always the smart thing to do. Before going to a new place, research the neighborhood prior to your visit. Performing a web search with the subject "Crime Reports" for a particular city or town will give you access to Police Department's crime reports, detailed city crime maps, and local hot spots (*See Appendix A: "Crime Report Information Sources for additional information and examples"*). Avoid persons or groups of persons that make you uneasy. Avoid dimly lit areas at night (e.g., parking lots, alleyways). Identify and steer clear of places where you could be ambushed. Avoid encounters and gatherings that could escalate to physical violence. If you find yourself in a bad situation, leave the area as soon as possible.

Awareness

- Awareness is the state of being conscious of one's immediate environment (being in the moment). Keep your eyes open, your head up, and always be aware of your surroundings. Most people are absorbed in thinking about the day's events at work or things that they need to do while out and about. Know the lay of the land and identify areas that may hide persons with bad intent. As you travel, identify escape routes so that you can extricate yourself if needed.

- Recognize problems in progress or beginning (coming/evolving). Use all of your senses to constantly scan for danger. Put the cell phone and earphones away, and **avoid distractions**. Being aware and present in your surroundings at all times is vital to avoiding possible surprise encounters.

Vigilance

Vigilance is the action or state of keeping careful watch for possible danger or difficulties. Take constant vigilance seriously. Use all of your senses, **look**, and **listen** for potential threats as part of your everyday routine. Practice scanning your surroundings three hundred sixty degrees as you travel. Be on the lookout to determine if someone is following you. When turning a corner at a building, go wide to ensure no one is lying in wait. When available, use reflective surfaces and shadows to observe your blind spots. Be keenly watchful and in the moment as you travel.

Body Language

- Body Language refers to the nonverbal signals that we use to communicate with each other. Even when they don't verbally express their thoughts, people constantly display clues to what they think and feel. From our facial expressions to our body movements, the things people do not say can still convey volumes of information.

- It is a fact that human predators select or reject potential victims quickly based on non-verbal and behavioral signals (body language). They look for the easy target (often women and the elderly). They observe potential targets from a distance and often approach to "test or interview" a potential victim assessing their level of confidence or submissiveness. The "Grayson/Stein Study" showed a consistent ability of a group of incarcerated violent offenders to select or reject the same individuals that had been video recorded on the street as targets (see "The Grayson/Stein Study" paragraph in "Victim Selection and What to Do About It – Toughen Up" in *Appendix B*). If, for example, you walk with your head down and shoulders slumped, you will be perceived as an easy target. Keep your head up, shoulders squared, and walk with confidence as a basic element of your travels.

- Being able to read and decode body language is useful in our daily interactions with others as well as identifying predators. It can be viewed as an early warning system helping to avoid troublesome encounters. Like any skill, learning to recognize and decode the meanings of body language requires practice (see "How to Decode Body Language to Spot a Predator" in *Appendix B.)*

- Of interest is the fact that individuals that have Self Defense Training in their background are less likely to be selected as a victim (see the first paragraph of "Victim Selection and What to Do About It" and the paragraph "The Preparation Equals Prevention Theory" in *Appendix B*).

- Learning how to Short Circuit the Victim Selection Process is an invaluable tool which should be an integral part of any Self-Defense System. There are several informative articles some which may be found in "Short Circuiting the Victim Selection Process" in *Appendix B*.

The book by Gavin de Becker, *The Gift of Fear* should be read by anyone interested in protecting themselves, particularly the female population.

Intuition

In the book, *The Gift of Fear,* by Gavin de Becker, he states that "It may be hard to accept its importance because intuition is usually looked upon by us thoughtful Western beings with contempt. It is often described as emotional, unreasonable, or inexplicable." While Intuition is generally attributed to females, the male version is going with the gut feeling. Most of us prefer to depend on logical thinking rather than going with our feelings. Intuition, or that gut feeling is a process that uses your life experiences, the entire range of your sensory inputs and body language as input within your subconscious to send you a warning to be wary. For example, if a stranger approaches you and something does not feel right, <u>LISTEN TO YOURSELF</u>. Take care not to dismiss the feeling as silly or unwarranted. The feeling may be one of caution or outright fear. In any situation, if you have the feeling that something does not feel right, listen to yourself and be on your guard.

If Approached by a Stranger

Avoiding dangerous situations includes what to do if approached by a stranger. Human predators observe potential targets from a distance and often approach them to assess their level of confidence and or submissiveness. They are looking for someone who is vulnerable and will allow themselves to be controlled. The stranger will likely appear to be nice and or charming. The first thing that you should ask yourself is, **"What do they want?"** What they want could be very bad for you. If your intuitive warning system is telling you something is wrong, pay attention. If the person becomes insistent, trying to offer help or prolong the encounter, **do not be afraid to be rude.** Exit the encounter as soon as possible. It is better to be thought of as rude than to become a victim. Obviously not every encounter will be accompanied by bad intent; perhaps they simply need directions.

Capable criminals are experts at keeping their victims from seeing warning signs that would expose their intent to manipulate and control them. The methods they employ can be used as "**tells**" to reveal their true intent. The following points outline the tells to look for. For an in-depth discussion of these tells, see Gavin de Becker's Book, *The Gift of Fear*, Chapter 4.

- <u>Charm/Niceness</u>: This tell usually occurs upon initial face-to-face contact. Keep in mind that a charming/nice stranger is neither charming nor nice. They are using charm and or friendliness because they want something from you. It may be quite innocent, although it may not be. If they offer to help you (carry your bags, open your car door), do not be afraid to refuse the offer. If someone is just being nice, they will most likely accept your refusal and move on. If they try to prolong the encounter, do not be afraid to be rude with your refusal. Tell them in a firm, raised voice to leave you alone if need be. It is better to be thought of as rude than to end up a victim.

- <u>Forced Teaming</u>: This tell is present when the stranger uses the word "we". The perpetrator attempts to elicit premature trust from the victim by making it hard for the victim to refuse without feeling rude and impolite. As an example, "We could get the bags into your apartment easily if I helped you." Once again, do not be afraid to be rude.

- <u>Too Many Details</u>: This tell is apparent when someone shares too many unnecessary details. When people are telling the truth, they do not feel the need to supply too many details. If what they have been saying does not sound credible to them, they keep talking to regain control. This tell usually occurs when they feel that their effort to control the intended victim is starting to fail.

- <u>Typecasting</u>: In this tell, the predator labels the victim in a slightly critical way hoping they will feel the need to prove that his opinion is not accurate. For instance, "You are too proud to accept help from someone like me." The victim feels the need to accept previously offered help to prove them wrong.

- <u>Loan Shark</u>: This tell occurs when the criminal offers to help the victim in such a way that the victim believes you owe them some type of reciprocal favor. The fact that you owe someone something makes it hard to ask to be left alone.

- <u>The Unsolicited Promise</u>: This tell is present when the predator promises to do something. Promises are used to convince the victim of an intention. The predator uses this method when they can see that you are not convinced of their intent. Ask yourself why they need to try to convince you. For example, if the criminal tells you he will leave after helping you put your bags in your apartment, his motive is almost always questionable.

- <u>Discounting the Word "NO"</u>: If a person repeatedly ignores or discounts the word NO in any of its forms (I do not need help, No thanks, I can take care of it….), they are either seeking to control you or refusing to lose any control they have established over you. Do not be afraid to be impolite or rude.

Running Away

It is Better to Avoid than to Run

It is Better to Run than to De-escalate

It is Better to De-escalate than to Fight

It is Better to Fight than to Die

While some may think of it as cowardly, running away is always a perfectly reasonable and smart choice to avoid conflict. Keep in mind that your survival and wellbeing are at stake once physical violence has begun. You do not know what the individual predator is capable of; they could have extensive hand-to-hand skills or have a weapon that could cause you great bodily harm. As you travel to different locations, identify where the exits are so that you may leave the area quickly if need be. If you are confronted in an isolated location, run to a well-populated area.

When in a group setting, such as a neighborhood bar, protest march, or political rally, there is always the possibility that a violent outbreak amongst different factions or points of view may ensue. You could easily find yourself a victim of a sucker punch or a thrown object. Remember, running away is always a perfectly reasonable and smart choice when available.

Walking Stick Self Defense

Facing Conflict

If confronted with physical violence, being able to defend yourself is key to your survival and wellbeing. Having a 'Self Defense Tool' like the Walking Cane/Stick readily at your disposal and knowing how to use it greatly helps to level the playing field in conflict, given no other choice. Keep in mind that it is safer to hand over your wallet or purse than confront someone with a superior weapon. Running away is always a perfectly reasonable and smart choice when available. The 'Walking Cane/Stick System' presented here is a simple and effective way to defend yourself against physical attacks when given no other choice. If violence is the only choice available, be prepared to fight for your life, survival, and wellbeing. You must remember that there is no such thing as a fair fight. Your goal in a violent physical altercation is to avoid or eliminate the threat as quickly as possible while surviving the encounter with as little personal damage as possible. The fight is only over once the assailant/assailants are completely neutralized, running away, and/or no longer a threat.

It is Better to Avoid than to Run

It is Better to Run than to De-escalate

It is Better to De-escalate than to Fight

It is Better to Fight than to Die

De-escalating Verbal Confrontations

Conflict often begins as an emotionally charged verbal confrontation. If not de-escalated, threats of violence or a direct move to physical violence may occur very quickly. If you find yourself in a verbal confrontation, raising your voice and participating in a shouting match will most certainly further inflame the emotional charge as will using insulting or threatening remarks. To de-escalate the confrontation, you will have to control your emotions and put your ego on hold. Maintaining a normal, calm level voice and non-threatening pose from the start will often de-escalate the emotional charge significantly. Your objective is to talk the perpetrator down from imminent threat to normal conversation using humor, apology, flattery, or logic as basic methods to steer the conversation in a direction that will defuse the situation.

As an example, consider the situation where you are seated in a restaurant and looking at the menu. You look up for an extended moment, deep in thought over a matter at work. A young man having dinner with his girlfriend gets up and angrily confronts you, wanting to know what kind of pervert you are. You hold your hands up, palms out, and apologetically and calmly explain that you were admiring the young lady's dress, explaining that you believe it would be the perfect gift for your wife's birthday and would like to know where it might be purchased.

Using apology and flattery in this example may well have de-escalated the confrontation. That said, you must always be alert and ready to react to violence if an attempt to de-escalate fails, resulting in imminent physical violence.

It is Better to Avoid than to Run

It is Better to Run than to De-escalate

It is Better to De-escalate than to Fight

It is Better to Fight than to Die

Physical Confrontation

The human predator views his victim as a resource. Their attack is a planned, efficient, and safe way for them to get what they want from the victim. Human predators generally use two distinct strategies to approach, control, or disable their victims.

1. In the first strategy, the predator attacks from ambush. They get as close to the victim as they can without being detected or triggering a defensive response. Once close to their target, they execute a brutal blitz attack catching the victim off guard. Being caught off guard generally results in the victim becoming temporarily shut down or frozen. In order to develop a response to this type of attack, specialized training is needed to enable the victim to counterattack immediately.

2. In the second strategy, the predator approaches the victim to start a conversation, usually employing charm or niceness. Their goal is to either get close enough to launch an overwhelming blitz attack or to gain control over the victim utilizing deceptive means or threats of violence. The targeted individual must recognize the verbal tells the predator uses to determine their intent. In order to keep the predator from closing distance, the targeted victim needs to utilize the environment along with Walking Stick keep away techniques covered in the following sections. Be on high alert at all times when confronted. If the predator pushes to close distance, you must take action immediately, responding to the imminent threat by running away or launching a counterattack.

If confrontation cannot be avoided, be focused and ready with your Walking Stick in the ready position. Be prepared to mount a **decisive blitz** **counterattack** **immediately** with the intent to end the encounter in a hurry (3 to 5 seconds). Your survival and wellbeing must be front and center as a single goal in mind. Clearly understand that you are in a fight for your life and wellbeing. Forego any fear of hurting the assailant. It is you or them; **make it them**. Use all of your tools (Walking Stick, hands, feet, legs, things you find in the environment, dirt to the eyes, rocks, bricks....) to quickly and efficiently neutralize the aggressor. Your job is not over until the threat no longer exists. Keep striking and blocking until you are confident about your safety.

- If you feel an altercation is moving toward an imminent attack, prepare yourself to react instantly.

- Once it is clear the altercation is headed to physical violence, bring the walking stick into a defensive and ready position.

- Be focused and ready to counter the threat instantly with a continuous series of strikes and blocks.

- From long or short-range, execute a series of strikes in a blitz manner (see striking patterns in the Striking section).

- Continue your counterattack using rapid strikes until the assailant is neutralized (either runs away or is incapacitated).

Physical Conflict preparedness training includes what to do as the situation evolves. Some of the tactics that complement effective self-defense are outlined in the following list of actions that should be practiced.

Shield/Barrier

If confronted with imminent physical confrontation, try to put a barrier between yourself and the assailant. This could be any physical object (a wall, pole, desk, car, planter, or a group of people).

Equalizer

Traveling with protective devices is always a good idea. The walking stick (aka walking cane) is an excellent choice as you can take it with you anywhere you travel legally. Whether it is a walking stick/cane, flashlight, pepper spray, knife, or firearm, ensure you are aware of the local laws and consequences of the levels of force implications when used. If you have no protective devices in your possession, many items at hand can be used as a deterrent or weapon. A stick, chair, newspaper, pencil, or rock can be used when confronted by someone either unarmed or equipped with a superior weapon. Anything in the environment can help to level the playing field.

Alliance

Seek help from friends or nearby persons who may be willing to help. It is always best to travel in pairs or more, especially in uncharted territory.

Fight to Survive

- Remember that the aim is to survive with as little damage to yourself as possible. This is not a video game; you will not respawn or gain full health immediately.

- There is no place for fairness in these situations. There is no such thing as a fair fight. It is you or them; make it them.

- With the laws of your present local in mind, be prepared to go beyond the consequences of your actions if need be. Your survival and wellbeing are paramount.

- Be pre-emptive if it is apparent that an attack is imminent (take the lead).

- Terminate the fight ASAP. Strive for a 3-second knockout (always use combinations of strikes in a 'Blitz' type attack).

- Be unconventional & unpredictable.

- Do not go to the ground if at all possible.

- It's only over when it's over (finish the fight). As long as you perceive the assailant is a threat, continue your counterassault.

- If necessary, **exit** the area of conflict when the opponent is down or disabled (Run if necessary).

Post Engagement Actions, When The Fight is Over

- Seek medical help if required. (Law Enforcement will likely become involved at this stage).

- Following any incident of defending yourself from a violent act, you must gather your thoughts and **immediately write up and or record the sequence of events in _minute detail._** A detailed record from start to finish should cover five essential elements found below that are generally needed to prove you acted in Self Defense. Include absolutely all hostile gestures, verbal or physical, and actions directed at and perceived by you from the protagonist. Recount your verbal phrases and interaction in attempting to de-escalate the situation. Record any witness information and write down their account of the altercation. If someone video-recorded the incident, get a copy for your records. Keeping a thorough and detailed record will help shield you from criminal and civil false allegations. Decide if contacting/or engaging the authorities/Law Enforcement is necessary or inevitable. **If needed, engage the services of a strong defense attorney who specializes in Self Defense Law.**

- From a general standpoint, Self-Defense is defined as the right to prevent suffering force or violence, while employing a sufficient level of counteracting force or violence. It's universally accepted that a person may protect themselves or others from harm under appropriate circumstances within the limits of regional Self Defense Laws, even when that behavior would normally constitute a crime. Although this sounds simple, actual situations raise many questions. For example, what is a sufficient level of force or violence when defending yourself? What goes beyond that level? What if the intended victim provoked the attack? Do victims have to retreat from the violence if possible? What happens when victims reasonably perceive a threat even if the threat does not actually exist? What if the victim's apprehension is subjectively genuine but objectively unreasonable? The specific rules and laws of your jurisdiction can be complicated.

The broad concepts that makeup self-defense law in the US are embodied in five essential elements. Note that all five elements must be proved. Any one of the elements disproved could end up with you found guilty of a crime.

  - Innocence: Legitimate Self Defense is only available if you, the innocent party to the confrontation. If you initiate or continue the confrontation when the perpetrator is down and no longer a threat, or running away, your actions cannot be justified as Self Defense and could be deemed criminal.

- o Imminence: An Imminent threat is one that is going to happen right now. The threat can be verbal so long as it puts the intended victim in immediate fear of physical harm. To prove "Imminence," it is essential to have a detailed account of the initial confrontation that led to violence.

- o Proportionality: Self-defense law requires the response of force or violence to be less than or equal to the level of the threat in question. In other words, a person can only employ as much force as required to remove the threat. If faced with deadly force, deadly force may be used to counter it. If faced with minor force, or deadly force claiming Self Defense will fail.

- o Avoidance: In the past, persons claiming Self-Defense had to try to avoid violence before using force. This was called the Duty To Retreat. While most states have removed this rule for instances involving nonlethal force, many states still require that a person attempt to escape the situation before applying lethal force.

  - ▪ In contrast to the duty to retreat, many states have enacted so-called Stand Your Ground laws. These laws remove the duty to retreat and allow for a claim of self-defense even if the claimant did nothing to flee from the threat of violence.

  - ▪ In states that require a person to retreat from the threat of imminent harm before defending themselves, a person can often use deadly force against someone who unlawfully enters their home. This rule, known as the Castle Doctrine, allows people to defend their homes against intruders through lethal force.

- o Reasonableness: Sometimes, Self-Defense is justified even if the perceived aggressor didn't mean harm to the perceived victim. Reasonableness is an umbrella element that covers the previously listed elements. Was your belief that you were defending yourself while initiating an attack, a reasonable belief proving innocence? Was it reasonable that the threat was imminent? Was your belief that you were using proportional force reasonable? What matters in these situations is whether a reasonable person in the same situation would have perceived an immediate threat of physical harm. As an example, if someone sees a wasp about to sting you and attempts to swat it away, you could reasonably conclude that they were assaulting you, triggering you to counterattack. While your actions taken to counter the perceived attack would normally be considered a criminal assault, you acted as any reasonable person would have. You would be judged as an instance of Self Defense.

Remember, after any instance of defending yourself from a violent act, you must gather your thoughts and **immediately write up and/or record the sequence of events in *minute detail*.** This record of the encounter will serve to protect you from civil litigation and provide a good attorney specializing in Self Defense law with the data needed to prove you acted in Self Defense.

For a further in-depth definition and clarification of the Five Essential Elements of Self-Defense Law, the book *The Law of Self Defense Principals* by Attorney Andrew F. Branca. may be obtained free of charge. *See Appendix H:* Self Defense Law.

The Self Defense Laws for individual states may be easily found on the web. *See Appendix H.* Self Defense Law for a couple of web search examples.

Choosing a Self Defense Walking Stick/Cane

Having a personal Self Defense Tool at your disposal and knowing how to use it effectively can greatly level the playing field if assaulted. Choosing a tool to fit your needs along with the training necessary to use it effectively, is of key importance. Know that whatever you choose, it should be legal to carry with you wherever and however you travel. Obviously, edged weapons and firearms are not going to be included. The overall category of Canes fits the need nicely. Canes are considered Assistive Medical devices and may be carried with you wherever and however you travel (*including air travel: See Appendix C:* Air Travel & TSA Information). The broad definition of the cane includes the Cane, Walking Cane, Walking Stick, and Assistive Cane. They are available in a variety of styles and shapes. Many of the styles can serve more than one purpose and or need of the individual. They are primarily used to aid **walking**, provide postural stability, balance, support, or assist in maintaining a **good posture**. Some designs serve as fashion accessories and/or a **Self Defense Tool.** When selecting a Cane as a Self Defense tool, several factors must be considered.

- If you intend to train in a Cane Self Defense system, the type of cane will be particular to that style.

- The Walking Cane/Stick's height is important to serve the dual purpose of a Self Defense and Assistive Mobility device. *See Appendix F:* Determining Walking Stick Height.

- Cane strength is important. You do not want to use a tool that may fail (break or bend) when used for practice or in confrontation.

- Cane weight should be chosen so that it may be swung easily.

- The Waking Stick/Cane should be durable.

- Canes differ primarily in the type of handle employed.

The basic cane has three parts which vary depending on the design of the cane and the intended use.

- The **handle** of a cane is extremely important and should be chosen to support the overall intended use. Many different styles exist, including but not limited to the **Tourist (or Crook) Handle**, the **Derby Handle,** and the **Knob Handle** (*See Cane Handle Styles in* Appendix D: Cane Handles)

Tourist (or Crook) Handle   **Derby/Fritz Handle**   **Knob Handle**

- The **shaft** of the cane transmits the load from the handle to the ferrule (tip). When choosing a cane, consider the shaft material strength, weight, and durability.

  - Traditional wood shafts are strong, with the durability driven by the type of wood. Some Canes designed specifically for self-defense may have notches cut into the shaft to enhance damage. Evidence has shown that these additions cause a weak spot that can, and has, caused the shaft to break.

  - Aluminum shafts are lightweight. Most Canes fabricated from aluminum are multi-piece adjustable or fold up canes.

  - Layered Fiberglass and Carbon Fiber shafts are very strong and extremely durable. Care must be exercised when making a choice as a thick shaft of this type may drive the weight so that it is ineffective for many users as a Self Defense tool.

  - The **Ferrule** or tip of a cane provides traction and added support. Many kinds of ferrules exist, but the most common is a simple rubber cap. Some designs include a brass Ferrule and a removable rubber cap. The rubber cap can easily be removed, exposing the brass cap to enhance thrusting effectiveness.

The Self Defense System presented here utilizes the Knob handle or Blunt Butt Cane. Throughout the remainder of the paper, this configuration shall be referred to as a **Walking Stick or a Walking Cane**. The techniques of the system are rooted in the Filipino Martial Arts where Stick, Edged weapons, and empty hand techniques are taught. The techniques presented here are generally applicable to other Cane configurations (Tourist/Rook and Derby/Fritz).

The vast majority of Cane Self Defense systems found on YouTube have been developed for the Crook handled cane. Some of the systems, like "Cane Masters," have developed techniques geared primarily to the style of the fighting cane they manufacture and market. These systems use the crook handle to hook the legs, arms, and neck to disrupt balance and pull the opponent to the ground. Some combat canes have ridges designed to inflict damage and a sharply pointed crook for piercing. The major difference between the **Walking Stick** system and crook handled systems are the hooking techniques. These techniques are advanced, taking a deal of time and training to be effective, depending on previous experience. Walking stick techniques are simple and effective.

For instructors and students of Filipino Martial Arts (FMA), the Walking Stick is basically just a longer stick. The addition of the two-handed grip techniques blends well with FMA single stick training.

We recommend purchasing a strong, lightweight model Walking Stick for everyday use. For durability, natural hard wood and composite shaft Walking Sticks are good choices. While convenient for travel, collapsible cane models are not durable and will likely fail if used for striking in an altercation. Be aware that some wood models on the market feature sharp grove notches cut into them to inflict additional damage. The notches may weaken the shaft or handle and have been known to cause a break upon impact at the cut (rounded notches do not present this issue). If you are looking for something fashionable or plain, choose what will be effective for your personal use. Note that aluminum Trekking poles, also known as Hiking Poles, are not considered Canes or Medical assistive devices. They may not be carried on aircraft as carry-on baggage; they must be checked in as baggage.

If you are looking for a Walking Stick that is both fashionable and effective, there are many choices. One favorite is the Irish Blackthorn Walking Stick. They are beautifully finished and feature a shaft that has natural Nubs along the length, which may be exploited to assist in ending attacks. A sturdy umbrella may also serve the need, although most models will fail after striking an opponent a few times. You may find umbrellas designed specifically for self-protection on the web (*Appendix E* Walking Stick Sources). These are expensive and somewhat limited by regional weather patterns. Strong effective walking sticks that may be used for self-protection are available online (*Appendix E* Walking Stick Sources). One favorite that we prefer and highly recommend is the **BlackSwift** Walking Stick/Cane. It is lightweight, durable, and reasonably priced.

You can fabricate your walking stick from wood or tree branches or by cutting the head off a golf club and adding a rubber cap to the end. For aircraft travel and general use, it is recommended that you use a purchased model rather than a homemade version. Depending on your physical condition and strength, a lightweight, sturdy walking stick is the easiest to handle. Regardless of your choice of a self-defense system and associated tool, you must realize that regular practice is necessary. Skills will fade if not practiced regularly. As with any physical endeavor, a reasonable level of physical fitness is required.

Basic Walking Stick Defense Concepts

The Walking Stick Self Defense system is based upon tried and true techniques utilized in the Doce Pares FMA (Filipino Martial Arts) system in which stick, knife, and empty hands are the primary weapons. The Walking Stick is a versatile self-defense tool. It can be used to keep an assailant at bay, block an assailant's strikes or grabs, and perform efficient striking counterattacks.

Walking Stick Grips

The way that the walking stick is gripped is important. The grips outlined in this section are simple and effective (except where specifically indicated). In all cases, the hands grab the stick with a fully closed fist. This is necessary in order to defend against having the stick easily pulled or knocked out of the hand in a confrontation.

Single-Handed Sword Grip

From the standing position with the hand on top of the walking stick (using the stick as a crutch), slide the hand forward, grasping the walking stick by the shaft, a hand's width distance from the ball end of the walking cane. This grip is suited for long-range striking and defense. Note that the free hand should be in a defensive position at face level.

Baseball Bat Grip

With one hand in the Single-Handed Sword Grip, the remaining hand grasps the stick adjacent to the first hand with the palms opposing. The Baseball Bat Grip can generate additional power when striking. The power is generated not only by swinging the walking stick with your arms, but it also utilizes your body motion (Turning into the strike) to amplify the power of your strike. This grip provides a powerful long-range striking and defense.

Right and Left-Handed Rifle Grip

With either hand in the Single-Handed Sword Grip, the remaining hand grasps the stick in the middle to one-quarter from the end of the walking with the palms opposing. This grip provides for effective short-range close-quarter striking and defensive techniques.

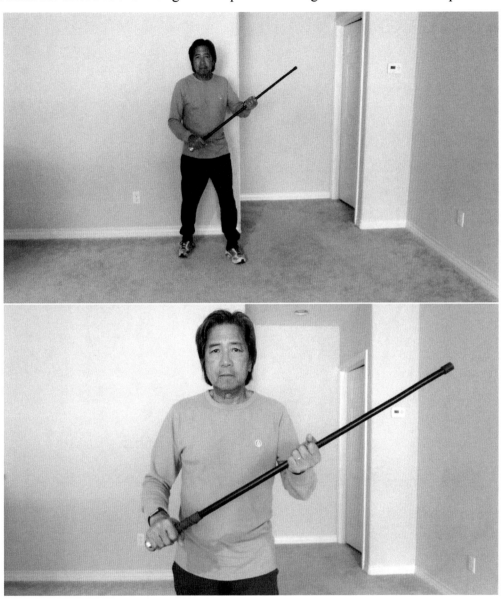

Bicycle Grip

In the Bicycle Grip, both hands are palm down and spaced evenly along the stick. This grip provides for effective short-range close quarter striking and defensive techniques.

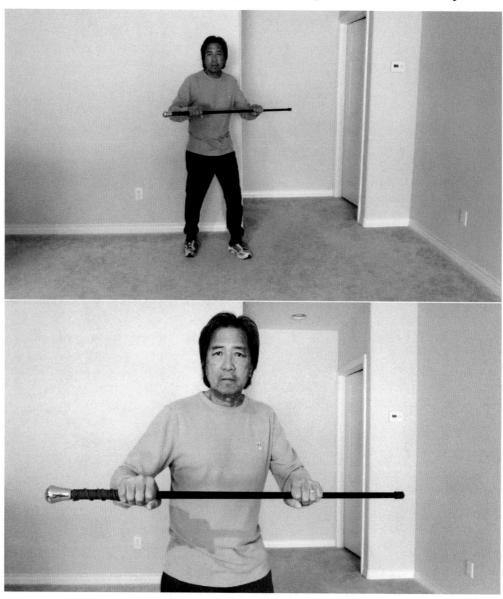

Single-Handed Reverse Sword Grip

(Not Recommended).

Two-handed Curl Grip

(Not Recommended).

Ranges

The distance from you to your opponent is defined as the "range" dictating the type of strike that can be used when defending oneself.

Long-Range:

While in Single-Handed Sword Grip or Baseball Bat Grip, long-range is defined as the point at which the tip of the walking stick may touch any point from an outstretched opponent's weapon or hand up to their body.

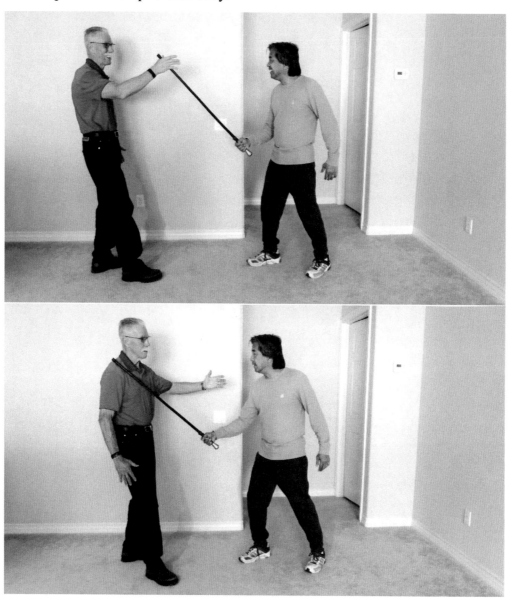

Short-Range:

While in Single-Handed Sword Grip, Baseball Bat Grip, Rifle Grip, or Bicycle Grip, short range is the point at which any portion of the walking stick or your hands may strike any point on the opponent's body. For short-range techniques, the Rifle or Bicycle grip is recommended. While short-range techniques can be used while in the Sword or Baseball Bat grip, it is very difficult to perform them due to the length of the Walking Stick.

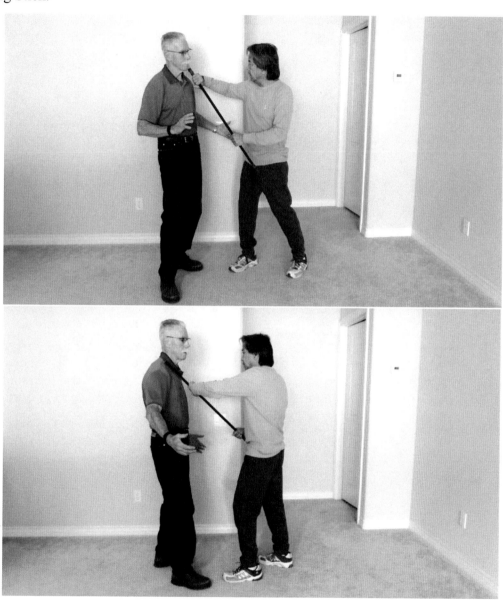

Neutral Positions:

When stationary, it is prudent to always have the walking stick positioned so that it may be employed for defensive action quickly and efficiently. It is best to hold the walking stick in a neutral non-threatening position; doing so will enable you to be ready to defend yourself while not appearing threatening to friendly folks.

Horizontal at Ease Stance:

With the Walking Stick in either the Bicycle or Rifle Grip. This is the recommended non-threatening at ease stance.

Horizontal Ready Stance.

If a potential threat is perceived, transition to the Horizontal Ready Stance for immediate implementation of effective blocking and striking. From the Horizontal at Ease Stance, lift the Walking Stick up to chest or shoulder level, ready to immediately implement effective blocking and striking.

Horizontal Reasonable Person Ready Stance.

From the Horizontal at Ease Stance, lift the Walking Cane up to head level. This position is used in conjunction with attempting to De-escalate an encounter. Using phrases like: "Wait a minute, let us talk this out" or "Hold on, I meant no disrespect". If the appeal for a peaceful solution is not accepted, you are ready to close your hands and defend yourself immediately.

Casual Crutch Stance:

Hand is on the heel of the stick (free hand ready in a non-threat position, topping crutch hand). This position is best suited for safe situations. If the situation changes to a possible threat, the stance should be changed to the Horizontal at Ease Stance.

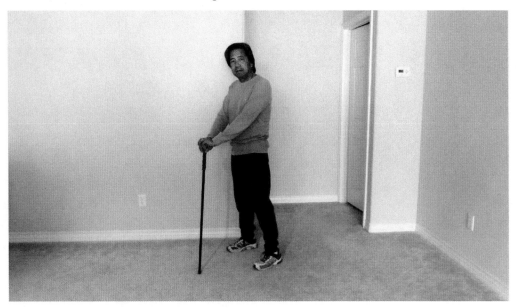

Crutch Stance:

Hand is on the heel of the stick (free hand ready in a non-threat position, crossed over to the other arm). This position is best suited for safe situations. If the situation changes to a possible threat, the stance should be changed to the Horizontal at Ease or Ready Stance.

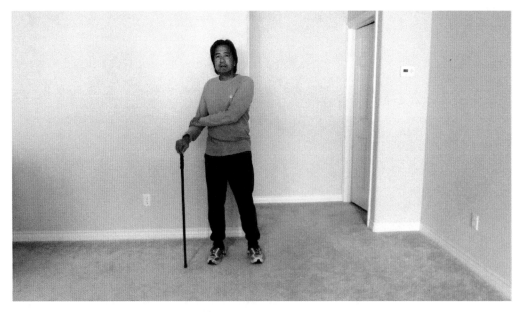

One Handed Crutch Stance:

Hand is on the heel of the stick (free hand hanging). This position should be **avoided** as the free hand is not readily employable for defensive action.

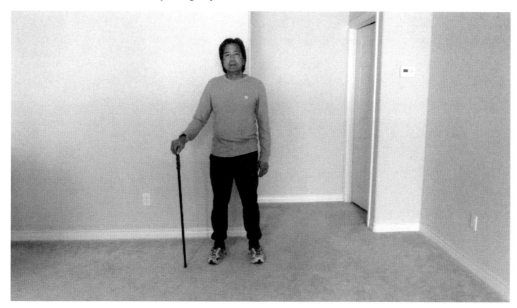

Hobo Stance:

Walking Stick is over the shoulder. This stance is **not recommended** unless used as a deterrent. Although the stance appears casual, the threat of a strike ready to be launched is obvious.

Striking

The Walking Cane system targets 12 striking areas, as depicted in Figure 1.

From any grip, the strikes are executed in a slashing or thrusting manner, contacting the target with the last 2 to 3 inches of either end of the Walking Cane.

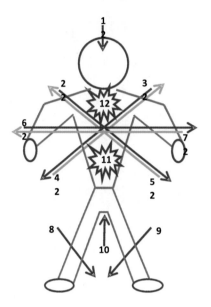

Figure 1. Strikes

Strike 1 is a downward vertical strike to the top of the forehead with the last 2 to 3 inches of the Cane.

Strike 2 is a downward diagonal strike with the last 2 to 3 inches of the cane from the opponent's right collarbone down to their left hip.

Strike 3 is a downward diagonal strike with the last 2 to 3 inches of the cane from the opponent's left collarbone down to their right hip.

Strike 4 is an upward diagonal strike with the last 2 to 3 inches of the cane from the opponent's right ribcage or hip up through their left collar bone.

Strike 5 is an upward diagonal strike with the last 2 to 3 inches of the cane from the opponent's left ribcage or hip up through their right collar bone.

Strike 6 is a horizontal strike from the opponent's right to left with the last 2 to 3 inches of the cane anywhere from the opponent's head to hip level.

Strike 7 is a horizontal strike from the opponent's left to right with the last 2 to 3 inches of the cane anywhere from the opponent's head to hip level.

Strike 8 is a downward diagonal strike with the last 2 to 3 inches of the cane to the opponent's right hip or leg.

Strike 9 is a diagonal downward strike with the last 2 to 3 inches of the cane from the opponent's left hip or leg.

Strike 10 is a thrust to the groin or bladder area.

Strike 11 is a thrust to the solar plexus.

Strike 12 is a thrust to the neck or face.

When in Sword Grip strikes 1 through 9 are slashes with the Tip or Butt End of the Walking Cane.

Sword Grip Tip End Slash

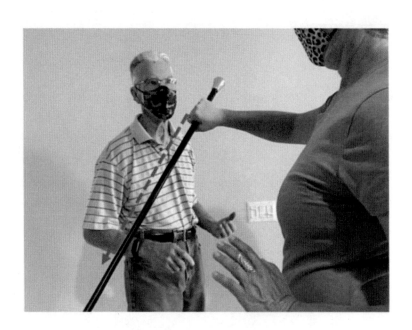

Sword Grip Butt End Slash

When in Sword Grip strikes 10, 11 & 12 are thrusts (stabs) with the tip or Butt End of the Walking Cane.

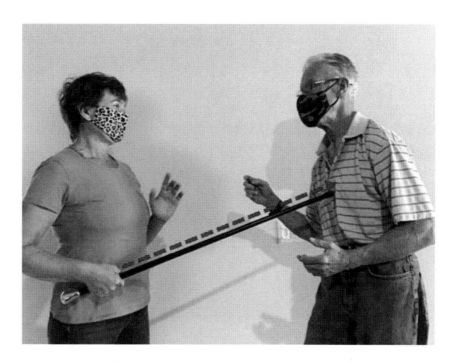

Sword Grip Tip End Thrust

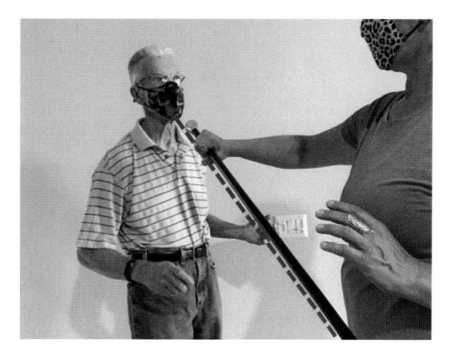

Sword Grip Butt End Thrust

When in Baseball Grip strikes 1 through 9 are slashes with the Tip or Butt End of the Walking Cane.

Baseball Grip Tip End Slash

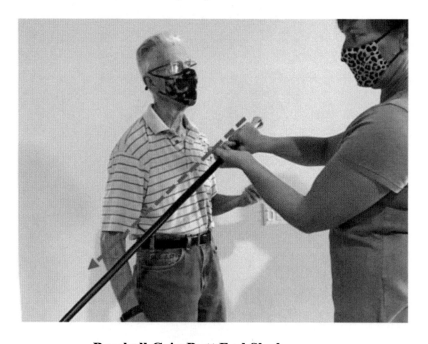

Baseball Grip Butt End Slash

When in Baseball Grip strikes 10, 11 & 12 are thrusts (stabs) with the Tip or Butt End of the Walking Cane.

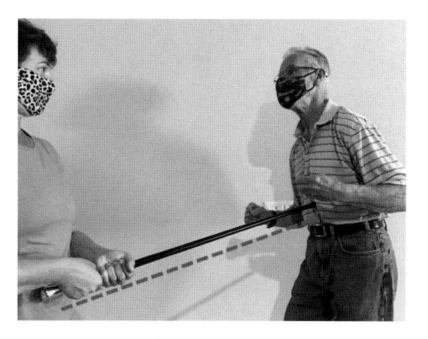

Baseball Grip Tip End Thrust

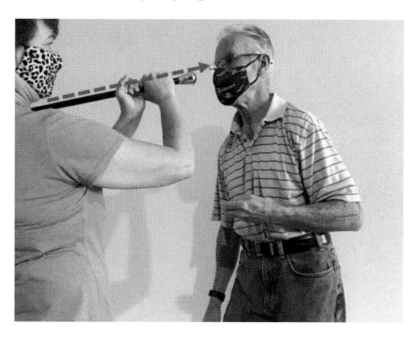

Baseball Grip Butt End Thrust

When in Rifle Grip strikes 1 through 9 are slashes with the Tip or Butt End of the Walking Cane.

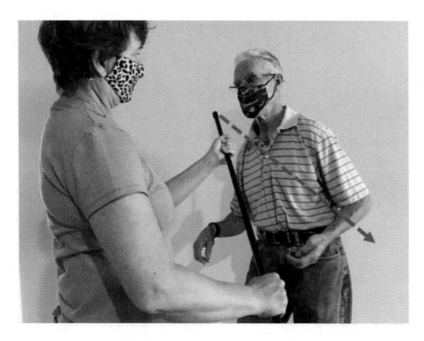

Rifle Grip Tip End Slash

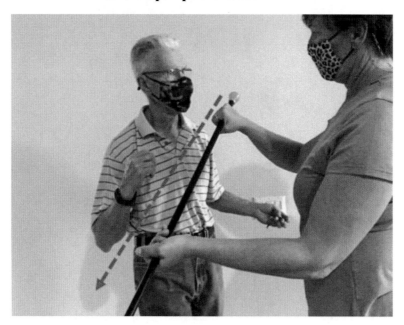

Rifle Grip Butt End Slash

When in Rifle Grip strikes 10, 11 & 12 are thrusts (stabs) with the Tip or Butt End of the Walking Cane.

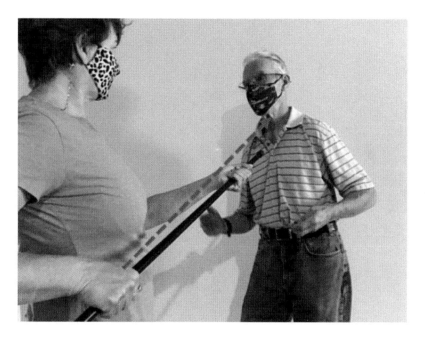

Rifle Grip Tip End Thrust

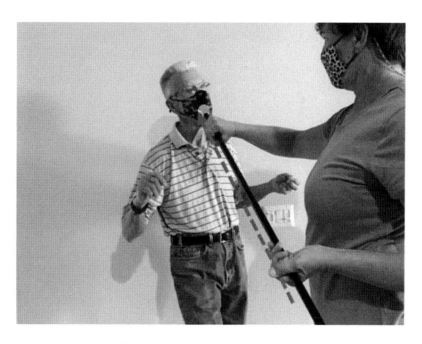

Rifle Grip Butt End Thrust

When in Rifle Grip strike 11 &12 may be executed as a horizontal Bunt Thrust with the mid section of the cane.

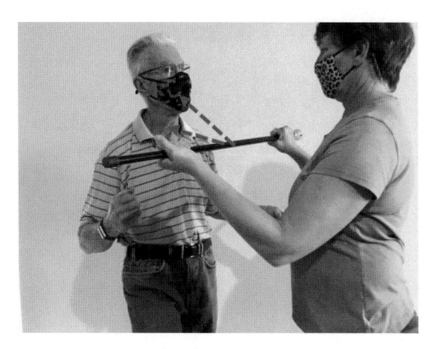

Rifle Grip Bunt Thrust

When in Bicycle Grip, strikes 1 through 9 are slashes with the Tip or Butt End of the Walking Cane.

Bicycle Grip Tip End Slash

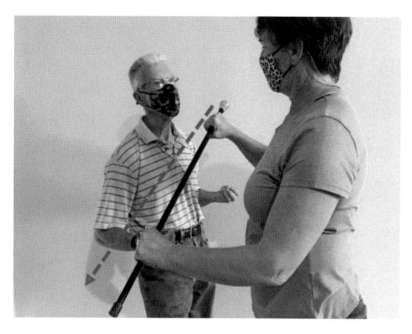

Bicycle Grip Butt End Slash

When in Bicycle Grip strikes 10, 11 & 12 are thrusts (stabs) with the Tip or Butt End of the Walking Cane.

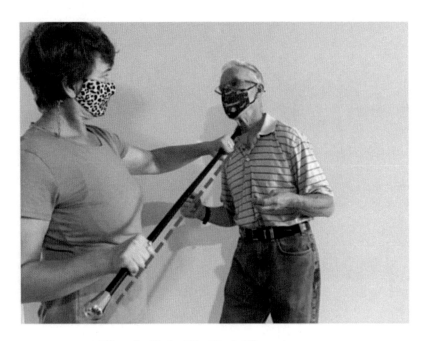

Bicycle Grip Tip End Thrust

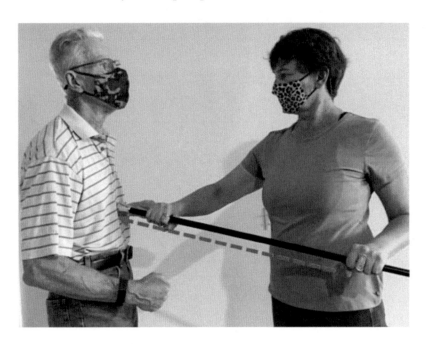

Bicycle But End Thrust

When in Bicycle Grip strike 11 & 12 may be executed as a horizontal Bunt Thrust with the mid section of the cane.

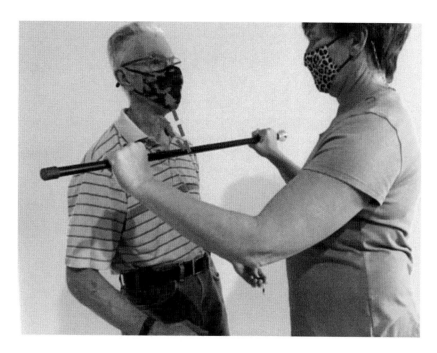

Bicycle Grip Bunt Thrust

Beginners Striking Exercises

These simple Striking exercises are designed to develop striking proficiency in a progressive manner. Execute the exercises using the Sword grip, Baseball grip, Bicycle grip, and the Rifle Grip. Be sure to advise students that while repetition is, at times, boring, it is necessary for the development of muscle memory. Following these simple striking exercises, progression to Zoning Footwork is introduced.

- Striking Exercise #1: As an introduction, execute strikes 1 through 12 standing in place. Odd numbered strikes will be executed with the butt end of the Walking Stick, while even numbered strikes will be executed with the tip end of the Walking Stick (Note that strikes 10, 11 & 12 may be executed with tip or butt end of the Walking Cane; for this exercise they follow the odd-even format)

- Striking Exercise #2: Execute strikes 1 through 12, stepping in place consecutively. Return to ready after each strike. (Performed independently with each of the Grips). Odd numbered strikes will be executed with the butt end of the Walking Stick, while even numbered strikes will be executed with the tip end of the Walking Stick.

  o Begin by assuming the Bicycle ready Stance (normal standing stance, feet parallel).

  o Step forward on odd-numbered strikes with the right foot. Return to the ready stance position.

  o Step forward on even-numbered strikes with the left foot. Return to the ready stance position.

  o Cycle through the exercise several times.

- Striking Exercise #3: Execute strikes 1 through 12, stepping forward and back in place consecutively. (Performed independently with all of the Grips). Odd numbered strikes will be executed with the butt end of the Walking Stick, while even numbered strikes will be executed with the tip end of the Walking Stick.

  o Begin by assuming the Bicycle Ready Stance.

  o Step forward with the right foot on odd-numbered strikes.

  o Step Back with the right foot on even-numbered strikes.

  o Execute the 12 strikes consecutively while stepping forward and back with the right foot.

  o Step back to the ready position after executing the 12 strikes.

- Striking Exercise #4: Execute strikes 1 through 12, continuously stepping forward through the 12 strikes. After Strike 12 has been completed, reverse the pattern by walking backward.

  o Begin by assuming the Bicycle Ready Stance.

  o Step forward with the right foot while executing Strike 1. Follow up by stepping forward with left foot executing Strike 2. Continue stepping forward right and left, executing Strikes 3 thru 12. Odd-numbered strikes are executed while stepping forward on the right foot, even-numbered strikes are executed while stepping forward on the left foot.

  o Stop after Strike 12 and assume Bicycle Ready Stance.

  o Step back with the left foot while executing Strike 1. Follow up by stepping back with the right foot executing Strike 2. Continue stepping back left and right, executing Strikes 3 thru 12. Odd-numbered strikes are executed while stepping back on the left foot, even-numbered strikes are executed while stepping back on the right foot. Repeat the exercise using the Baseball grip, Bicycle grip, and Rifle Grip.

- Striking Exercise #5: Execute strikes 1 through 12 continuously in sets of three forward and three back. Odd numbered strikes will be executed with the butt end of the Walking Stick while even numbered strikes will be executed with the tip end of the Walking Stick.

  o Begin by assuming the Bicycle Ready Stance.

  o Step forward with the right foot while executing Strike #1. Step forward with the left foot while executing Strike #2. Step forward with the right foot while executing Strike #3.

  o Step back with the right foot while executing Strike #4. Step back with the left foot while executing Strike #5. Step back with the right foot while executing Strike #6.

  o Step forward with the right foot while executing Strike #7. Step forward with the left foot while executing Strike #8. Step forward with the right foot while executing Strike #9.

  o Step back with the right foot while executing Strike #10. Step back with the left foot while executing Strike #11. Step back with the right foot while executing Strike #12.

  o Return to the Bicycle ready Stance.

Repeat the exercise using the Baseball grip, Bicycle grip, and Rifle Grip.

Intermediate Level Striking Exercises

Some of the next set of Striking Exercises include turning, which may be challenging for some students, balancing wise. Prior to covering these exercises, students should practice the turning methods outlined in the Turning and Pivoting Section. The instructor should evaluate each student's balance stability to determine the best method for the individual.

- Striking Exercise #6: Execute strikes 1 through 12 continuously in sets of three, turning 180 degrees after each set of 3 strikes. Note that the turn called out here is the Hook Step Turn, which may be replaced by any other turning methods found in the Turning Section. Odd-numbered strikes will be executed with the butt end of the Walking Stick, while even-numbered strikes will be executed with the tip end of the Walking Stick.

  o Begin by assuming the Bicycle Ready Stance.

  o Step forward with the right foot while executing Strike #1. Step forward with the left foot while executing Strike #2. Step forward with the right foot while executing Strike #3.

  o Hook Step Turn.

  o Step forward with the left foot while executing Strike #4. Step forward with the right foot while executing Strike #5. Step forward with the left foot while executing Strike #6.

  o Hook Step Turn.

  o Step forward with the right foot while executing Strike #7. Step forward with the left foot while executing Strike #8. Step forward with the right foot while executing Strike #9.

  o Hook Step Turn.

  o Step forward with the left foot while executing Strike #10. Step forward with the right foot while executing Strike #11. Step forward with the left foot while executing Strike #12.

  o Return to the Bicycle ready Stance.

Repeat the exercise using the Baseball grip, Bicycle grip, and Rifle Grip.

- Striking Exercise #7: Execute strikes 1 through 12 continuously in sets of three forward and 3 back with Grip Changes.

    o Begin by assuming the Bicycle Ready Stance.

    o Change to Sword Grip, step forward with the right foot, and execute Strike #1. Step forward with the left foot while executing Strike #2. Step forward with the right foot while executing Strike #3.

    o Change to Bicycle Grip, stepping back with the right foot while executing Strike #4. Step back with the left foot while executing Strike #5. Step back with the right foot while executing Strike #6.

    o Change to Baseball Grip, stepping forward with the right foot while executing Strike #7. Step forward with the left foot while executing Strike #8. Step forward with the right foot while executing Strike #9.

    o Change to Rifle Grip, stepping back with the right foot while executing Strike #10. Step back with the left foot while executing Strike #11. Step back with the right foot while executing Strike #12.

    o Return to the Bicycle ready Stance.

- Striking Exercise #8: Execute strikes 1 through 12 continuously in sets of three, turning 180 degrees after each set of 3 strikes. Note that turn called out here is the Hook Step Turn which may be replaced by any of the other turning methods found in the Turning Section.

    o Begin by assuming the Bicycle Ready Stance.

    o Change to Sword Grip, stepping forward with the right foot while executing Strike #1. Step forward with the left foot while executing Strike #2. Step forward with the right foot while executing Strike #3.

    o Hook Step Turn.

    o Change to Bicycle Grip, stepping forward with the left foot while executing Strike #4. Step forward with the right foot while executing Strike #5. Step forward with the left foot while executing Strike #6.

    o Hook Step Turn.

    o Change to Baseball Grip, stepping forward with the right foot while executing Strike #7. Step forward with the left foot while executing Strike #8. Step forward with the right foot while executing Strike #9.

    o Hook Step Turn.

    o Change to Rifle Grip, stepping forward with the left foot while executing Strike #10. Step forward with the right foot while executing Strike #11. Step forward with the left foot while executing Strike #12.

    o Return to the Bicycle ready Stance.

Zoning

Zoning is an important component of effective blocking and striking. It results in three important advantages:

- When blocking, Zoning moves your head and body offline from the opponent's Strike or attempted grab.

- It removes you from the opponent's Power zone, weakening their strikes.

- It isolates the opponent's far-side hand, effectively shutting down its use for defense or offence momentarily.

A simple drill to teach proper Zoning starts with two sticks laid out on the floor in a V pattern 90 degrees apart, with the vertex pointing directly toward the student.

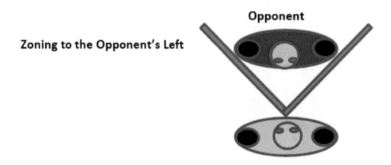

With the opponent directly in front of you, step on a 45 degree angle to the opponent's left side with your right foot, dragging the left foot to the right into a stable stance facing the opponent's left side.

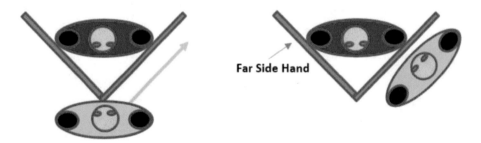

After Zoning, you are to the opponent's left side with both of your hands accessible for Blocking and Striking.

Showing a diagram like the one above to students having difficulty with Zoning has been useful.

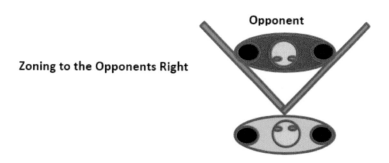

Opponent

Zoning to the Opponents Right

With the opponent directly in front of you, step on a 45 degree angle to the opponent's right side with your left foot, dragging the right foot to the left into a stable stance facing the opponent's side.

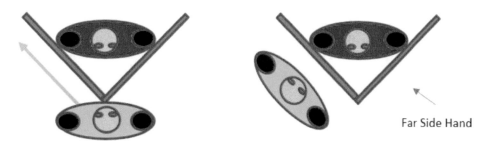

Far Side Hand

After Zoning, You are to the opponent's right side with both of your hands accessible for Blocking and Striking.

Turning and Pivoting

Being able to turn around 180 degrees, or pivot to 90 degrees to face another direction while maintaining a good balance, can be difficult for some. It is particularly difficult for those with limited range of motion, balance, or gait issues, including many seniors. Turning or pivoting while maintaining good balance is important when confronted with a threat from another direction.

Any of the methods presented here may be adapted to pivoting less than 180 degrees by simply truncating the pivot to face the desired direction. When turning, always look in the direction of the turn. The turn begins with the foot that corresponds to the direction of the turn. This movement may be as simple as pivoting the foot slightly in the direction of the turn. For balance-challenged individuals, the instructor should work with the student to determine the most stable turning and pivoting method.

- Crossing Step Forward Pivot Turn: **In order to execute this turn step forward, crossing over the center line and pivot on both feet.**

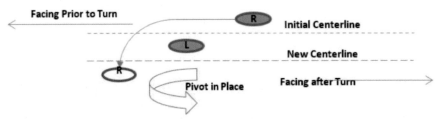

- Hook Step Turn: **In order to execute this turn, step rear foot across the back of the forward foot (rear shin touches front leg calf) and pivot on both feet.**

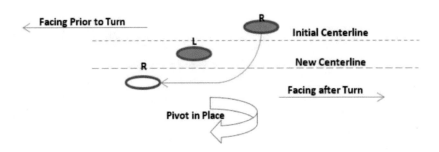

- **Front Foot Step Across Turn:** In order to execute this turn, step front foot horizontally across, and pivot on both feet-180 Degrees in place. Note:

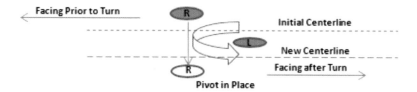

- **Karate Turn:** In order to execute this turn, look over the shoulder in the direction of turn (Rear Foot). Step rear foot horizontally across. Pivot 180 Degrees in place. Pivot In place stepping to the side with the rear (new front) foot.

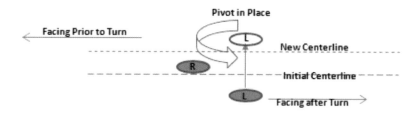

- **Walk Around Four Step Turn:** While this method executes a slower turn, it is more stable for balance challenged individuals. To execute a right turn, step to the right with the right foot first and simply walk around 180 degrees in four steps. Turning to the left is executed in the same manner with the steps to the left.

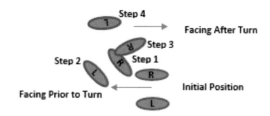

Turning and Pivoting Exercises

This exercise has the student turn or pivot to face an approaching threat from a random direction. Let them imagine that an off leash dog is rapidly approaching from an unspecified direction.

With the student facing the 12:00 position on a clock face, call out a variety of clock numbers having the student pivot so that they are facing that direction. Once they are facing the direction specified by the number, have them reset back to the starting 12:00 position prior to calling out a new number. Start slowly, using only the 12, 3, 6, and 9 positions. As the student becomes more confident, have them execute the exercise using all directions relative to the clock face. As a further challenge, have the student execute the exercise from their current called orientation without resetting to the 12:00 position:

- With the current orientation of the clock face is assumed to be fixed.

- With the clock face assumed to have realigned 12:00 to be straight in front of them.

As an exercise in a group class setting, have one student stand in the middle of a circle of fellow students who are aligned with the clock face scheme. The instructor will call out a clock number to which the student in the middle will turn or pivot to. If there is a fellow student in that position, they will execute a random strike. The student in the middle will block the strike and be ready for the next strike. The orientation of the imagined clock face now changes such that 12:00 is reset to the current direction the student in the middle faces. The student in the middle will block the strike and be ready for the next strike.

The simple block by the student in the middle may be replaced with a block followed by three or more counterstrikes or a block followed by three or more counterstrikes and a disarm.

Striking Exercises Utilizing Zoning

<u>Striking Exercise #1</u>: Execute strikes 1 through 12, stepping in place consecutively. (Performed independently with each of the Grips)

- Begin by assuming the Bicycle Ready Stance.

- Step directly forward, executing Strike 1 with the Butt end of the Walking Cane.

- Return to the Bicycle Ready Stance.

- Zone to the left executing Strike 2 with the Tip end of the Walking Cane.

- Return to the Bicycle Ready Stance.

- Zone to the right executing Strike 3 with the Butt end of the Walking Cane.

- Return to the Bicycle Ready Stance.

- Zone to the left executing Strike 4 with the Tip end of the Walking Cane.

- Return to the Bicycle Ready Stance.

- Zone to the right executing Strike 5 with the Butt end of the Walking Cane.

- Return to the Bicycle Ready Stance.

- Zone to the left executing Strike 6 with the Tip end of the Walking Cane.

- Return to the Bicycle Ready Stance.

- Zone to the right executing Strike 7 with the Butt end of the Walking Cane.

- Return to the Bicycle Ready Stance.

- Zone to the left executing Strike 8 Stance with the Tip end of the Walking Cane.

- Return to the Bicycle Ready Stance.

- Zone to the right executing Strike 9 Stance with the Butt end of the Walking Cane.

- Return to the Bicycle Ready Stance.

- Zone to the left executing Strike 10. with the Tip end of the Walking Cane.

- Return to the Bicycle ready Stance.

- Zone to the right executing Strike 11 with the Butt end of the Walking Cane.

- Return to the Bicycle Ready Stance.

- Zone to the left executing Strike 12. with the Tip end of the Walking Cane

- Return to the Bicycle Ready Stance.

Single Grip Strike Sequences

As with any Self Defense system, practicing regularly is necessary. Practicing striking sequences will allow the student to flow from strike to strike efficiently. The sequences should be practiced with all grips. When possible, the strikes should be executed facing a partner in striking range. Keeping safety in mind, ensure that the strikes performed would actually hit the targeted area if followed through. This will foster proper targeting for the strikes. Note that in all cases, the last 3 inches of the Walking Cane (Tip or Butt) should be the point of contact as that will exert the maximum amount of force for the strike. These combinations may also be used as a basic bag routine.

Note that the student is to execute a Right or Left zone prior to the first strike. If needed, these exercises may be used for beginners without zoning.

- Strike Sequence # 1 (4 Strikes)
  - Zone Right
  - Strike #3 with the Butt end of the Walking Cane.
  - Strike #6 with the Tip end of the Walking Cane.
  - Strike #9 with the Butt end of the Walking Cane.
  - Strike #4 with the Tip end of the Walking Cane.

- Strike Sequence # 2 (4 Strikes)
  - Zone Left
  - Strike #8 with the Tip end of the Walking Cane.
  - Strike #7 with the Butt end of the Walking Cane.
  - Strike #2 with the Tip end of the Walking Cane.
  - Strike #5 with the Butt end of the Walking Cane.

- Strike Sequence # 3 (4 Strikes)
  - Zone Right
  - Strike #7 with the Butt end of the Walking Cane.
  - Strike #2 with the Tip end of the Walking Cane.
  - Strike #3 with the Butt end of the Walking Cane.
  - Strike #12 with the Tip end of the Walking Cane.

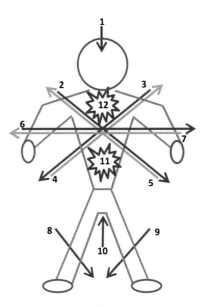

- Strike Sequence # 4 (4 Strikes)
  - Zone Left
  - Strike # 2 with the Tip end of the Walking Cane.
  - Strike #9 with the Butt end of the Walking Cane.
  - Strike #4 with the Tip end of the Walking Cane.
  - Strike #12 with the Tip end of the Walking Cane.

- Strike Sequence # 5 (4 Strikes)
  - Zone Right
  - Strike #4 with the Tip end of the Walking Cane.
  - Strike #12 with the Tip end of the Walking Cane.
  - Strike #3 with the Butt end of the Stick.
  - Strike #11 with the Butt end of the Walking Cane.

- Strike Sequence # 6 (4 Strikes)
  - Zone Left
  - Strike #6 with the Tip end of the Walking Cane.
  - Strike #1 with the Butt end of the Walking Cane.
  - Strike #8 with the Tip end of the Walking Cane.
  - Strike #10 with the Tip end of the Walking Cane.

- Strike Sequence # 7 (5 Strikes)
  - Zone Right
  - Strike #1 with the Butt end of the Walking Cane.
  - Strike #2 with the Tip end of the Walking Cane.
  - Strike #7 with the Butt end of the Walking Cane.
  - Strike #8 with the Tip end of the Walking Cane.
  - Strike #10 with the Tip end of the Walking Cane.

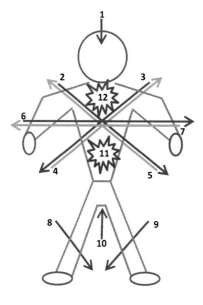

- Strike Sequence # 8 (5 Strikes)
  - Zone Left
  - Strike #6 with the Tip end of the Walking Cane.
  - Strike #9 with the Butt end of the Walking Cane.
  - Strike #2 with the Tip end of the Walking Cane.
  - Strike #7 with the Butt end of the Walking Cane.
  - Strike #1 with the Tip end of the Walking Cane.

- Strike Sequence # 9 (5 Strikes)
  - Zone Right
  - Strike #7 with the Butt end of the Walking Cane.
  - Strike #6 with the Tip end of the Walking Cane.
  - Strike #3 with the Butt end of the Walking Cane.
  - Strike #2 with the Tip end of the Walking Cane.
  - Strike #11 with the Tip end of the Walking Cane.

- Strike Sequence # 10 (5 Strikes)
  - Zone Left
  - Strike #2 with the Tip end of the Walking Cane.
  - Strike #3 with the Butt end of the Walking Cane.
  - Strike #12 Butt with the Butt end of the Walking Cane.
  - Strike #1 with the Tip end of the Walking Cane.
  - Strike #12 with the Tip end of the Walking Cane.

Encourage the student to try combinations of their own that flow easily!

Grip Changing Striking Sequences

During conflict, the distance to the opponent can change quickly. Be ready to adjust your grip to cover short and long ranges.

- Grip Changing Striking Sequence # 1

  o At long-range from Bicycle Grip, raise the Walking Cane to chest level.

  o Release the Walking Cane from left hand, transitioning to right-hand Sword Grip followed immediately with Strike #6.

  o Follow up in Sword Grip with Strike #3, pulling all the way through.

  o Switch to Bicycle Grip, step forward with left foot into the target immediately executing Strike #4 with the tip end of the Walking Stick.

  o Follow up immediately with Strike #12 to the face with tip end of the Walking Stick.

  o Step back with left foot transitioning to Sword Grip and execute Strike #1.

  o Switch to Rifle Grip, stepping forward with left foot executing Strike #11.

- Grip Changing Striking Sequence # 2

  o At long-range from Bicycle Grip, raise Walking Cane to chest level.

  o Stepping forward with left foot, execute a horizontal smash to the face of the opponent, pushing them back to long-range.

  o Transition to Sword Grip, step back with left foot executing Strike #6.

  o Follow up immediately with Strike #1.

  o Transition to Rifle Grip, stepping forward with left foot executing Strike #12 with tip end of the Walking Stick.

  o Follow up immediately by stepping forward with right foot executing Strike #5 with the butt end of the Walking Stick.

  o Transition to Baseball Grip, step back with right foot executing Strike #2.

  o Follow up Immediately, stepping forward with right foot executing Strike #7.

Encourage the student to try combinations of their own that flow easily for them.

Blocking, Parrying, and Redirecting Opponent Strikes and Grab Attempts

When in Close Range, the opponent's strikes and grabs are best countered from the Rifle or Bicycle Grip. When a punch or grab is attempted, the walking stick is used to block, parry, or redirect the incoming threat. The defender should always attempt to maneuver (zone) to one side or the other of the attacker's body such that the opposite hand is out of play.

Outside Block:

As an individual with the potential intent to attack approaches transition from a Horizontal at Ease stance to Horizontal Ready Stance.

From the Horizontal Ready Stance.

Zone to the outside, executing a forceful block. The stick should be at a 45 to 90 degree angle.

Push the block by turning the opponent as far as possible, isolating their off arm so that it is out of play.

Immediately execute a blitz of strikes. A head thrust is usually readily available.

Inside Block with Rollover Redirect

While blocking to the outside is preferred, there are times in engagement when you may have to execute an inside block. In these instances, one should efficiently get to the outside as soon as possible.

As an individual with the potential intent to attack approaches transition from Horizontal at Ease stance to Horizontal Ready Stance.

Prepare to meet the potential threat from horizontal ready by starting to zone.

Finding yourself inside the opponent's attack block forcefully.

From the block position, begin to execute a rollover to the outside.

While executing the block, take advantage of striking opportunities if available.

Begin to rotate the Walking Cane about its center such that the tip of the Walking Cane in this case is rotated up and the butt is rotated down with the center of the Walking Cane on the attacker's arm rotated down (hidden from view on another side).

As the Walking Cane is rotated, lift the opponent's arm up and over while zoning to the outside.

Continue pushing the opponent's arm in an arc you are outside.

When you have rotated to the outside push the opponent's arm forcefully, turning the opponent so that their back is exposed.

Immediately Execute a blitz of strikes.

Outside Block of Double Hand Grab Attempt

In the event that the opponent approaches reaching with both hands with the potential intent to attack, transition from Horizontal at Ease stance to Horizontal Ready Stance.

Be ready to meet the threat.

Zone to the outside and forcefully block.

Push through the block to expose the opponent's back.

Vigorously pushing all the way through helps to turn the opponent and will likely affect their balance. Immediately execute a blitz of strikes.

Inside Block with Hooking Redirect

In the event that the opponent approaches with potential intent to attack transition from Horizontal at Ease stance to Horizontal Ready Stance.

Execute a forceful block.

Hook over opponent's arm with the end of the walking Stick that is currently up as a result of the block.

Pull through, exposing the opponent's back.

Push all the way through.

Execute a blitz of strikes.

Two Hand Grab Attempt Face Smash

As the opponent reaches with both hands, move the Walking Cane to high ready.

Raise the Walking Stick to jump over the attacker's arms.

Slam down on the opponent's arms forcefully.

Execute horizontal smash to face. Follow up with a flurry of strikes.

Counter Attack Exercises

When an opponent attacks with either a strike or grab attempt, transitioning from your immediate defensive response with a barrage of counterstrikes must commence immediately. These Counter Attack Exercises will form a basis for effective flowing strike sequences after initially blocking, parrying, redirecting, or checking the opponent's attack. In order to simulate a confrontation with an aggressor, have the student start at a low ready position (Walking Cane in Bicycle Grip, arms straight down), shifting to a high ready position as an attack is expected (Walking Stick in Bicycle Grip at chest level). Upon simulated strike or grab by the aggressor with right, left, or both hands, have the student execute one of the series of Block/Parry strike sequences. Ensure the block is executed with the Walking Stick at a 45 to 90 degree angle. It is suggested that students work in pairs at a slow pace to practice the combinations, aggressor/defender. Once they have gained experience with the sequences, have the 'aggressor' present random strikes/grabs with the defender using efficient flowing combinations (figure 8 striking) in response. For individual practice, have the student work the exercises on a bag and/or shadow blocking and striking. Obviously, there are many other efficient blocking and striking combinations that are possible. Have the student work on additional combinations that are efficient and flow smoothly using the figure-eight concept. These exercises are foundational to the 3 to 5 second Knock Out concept.

Outside Block Exercises

- Block/Parry Strike Sequence # 1

  - Aggressor attempts a right-hand strike/grab.

  - Zone left executing an outside block, followed up immediately with a blitz of strikes utilizing a figure 8 pattern.

  - Strike #12: Tip end.

  - Strike #3: Ball end.

  - Strike #6: Tip end.

  - Strike #5: Ball end.

  - Strike #12: Ball end.

- Block/Parry Strike Sequence # 2

  - Aggressor attempts a left-hand strike/grab.

  - Zone right executing an outside block followed up immediately with a blitz of strikes utilizing a figure 8 pattern.

  - Strike #12: Ball end.

  - Strike #4: Tip end.

  - Strike #5 Ball end.

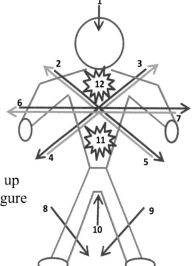

- o Strike # 6 Tip end.
- o Strike #11 Tip end.
- Block/Parry Strike Sequence # 3
  - o Aggressor attempts a right-hand strike/grab.
  - o Zone left executing an outside block, followed up immediately with a blitz of strikes utilizing a figure 8 pattern.
  - o Strike #12: Tip end.
  - o Strike #7: Ball end.
  - o Strike #8: Tip end.
  - o Strike #10: Tip end.
  - o Strike #11: Tip end.
- Block/Parry Strike Sequence # 4
  - o Aggressor attempts a left-hand strike/grab.
  - o Zone right executing an outside block, followed up immediately with a blitz of strikes utilizing a figure 8 pattern.
  - o Strike #12: Ball end.
  - o Strike #6: Tip end.
  - o Strike #9: Ball end.
  - o Strike #10: Ball end.
  - o Strike #12: Ball end.
- Block/Parry Strike Sequence # 5
  - o Aggressor attempts a right-hand strike/grab.

- Zone left executing an outside block, followed up immediately with a blitz of strikes utilizing a figure 8 pattern.
    - Strike #2: Tip end.
    - Strike #12: Tip end.
    - Strike #7: Ball end.
    - Strike #8: Tip end.
    - Strike #10: Tip end.

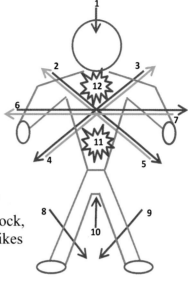

- Block/Parry Strike Sequence # 6
    - Aggressor attempts a left-hand strike/grab.
    - Zone right executing an outside block, followed up immediately with a blitz of strikes utilizing a figure 8 pattern.
    - Strike #3: Ball end.
    - Strike #4: Tip end.
    - Strike #7: Ball end.
    - Strike #2: Tip end.
    - Strike #12: Tip end.

- Block/Parry Strike Sequence # 7
    - Opponent performs a right-hand strike/grab.
    - Zone left executing an outside block, followed up immediately with a blitz of strikes utilizing a figure 8 pattern.
    - Strike #5: Ball end.
    - Strike #6: Tip end.
    - Strike #3: Ball end.
    - Strike #11: Ball end.
    - Strike #4: Tip end.

- Block/Parry Strike Sequence # 8

  o Opponent attempts a left-hand strike/grab.

  o Zone right executing an outside block, followed up immediately with a blitz of strikes utilizing a figure 8 pattern.

  o Strike #4: Tip end.

  o Strike #7: Ball end.

  o Strike #2: Tip end.

  o Strike #10: Tip end.

  o Strike #5: Ball end.

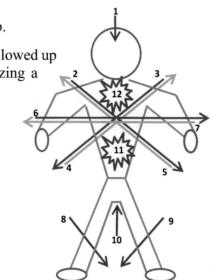

The 3 to 5-Second Knockout

The concept of the 3 to 5 Second Knockout is to end an altercation quickly with as little damage to yourself as possible. When approached by a person who you view as a potential threat, you should always assume a defensive posture. The Bicycle grip held at chest level is preferred. This non-threatening posture allows for a quick reaction if the aggressor initiates an attempted strike or grab. Once the aggressor has initiated a grab, strike, or forward advance, you are in close range. Meeting the advance of the opponent head-on facilitates the execution of a 3 to 5-second knockout. The natural reaction by untrained individuals is to retreat to long-range. This action will likely prolong the encounter and may give the opponent an advantage. Be aware that once the aggressor has committed, it is highly likely that they will continue to advance and work to gain an advantage. While most people may feel uncomfortable this close to the aggressor, it needs to be understood and stressed that this is where the action will take place. As soon as the aggressor advances (grab, punch, or step forward), immediately execute a block/parry, followed by a continual blitz of strikes. The Block/Parry and Counter-Strike Sequences covered in the previous section are examples of sequences to use. They are intended to teach the student to move from blocking and striking in a continuous flowing manner. As with any confrontation, no one sequence of moves or techniques will ensure success. Physical conflict is dynamic and unpredictable. You must be ready to change your actions based on your opponent's presence. If you start a series of well-trained strikes after a block, you may have to block an additional strike and move on to another series of strikes based on the actions of the opponent. Do not stop until the threat is nullified. Practicing safely with a partner, have the aggressor present challenges such that the defender has to continuously block and strike in a flowing figure 8 manner. Ensure to target vital areas (head, throat, kidney) as well as the extremities.

- Be ready: Stick in Bicycle Grip at chest level.

- Block or parry incoming strikes or grab attempts.

- When possible, Zone and use outside blocks to position to the side or rear of the opponent, negating one of their arms.

- Execute a series of strikes in blitz fashion.

- Be ready to counter additional strikes or grabs.

- Be unpredictable. You do not want to execute the same pattern over and over, giving the opponent the advantage of knowing what is next.

- Use a combination of slashing strikes and thrusts (Strikes 10, 11, and 12).

- Three to five seconds is a short time period. It will seem to last forever when in action.

Making Space or Keeping the Assailant Away:

There may be instances where you need to keep an opponent at bay or open up space between you and your assailant while trying to defuse an encounter or to make <u>distance</u> for efficient striking.

- **Hobo Stance**: To casually warn off individuals, assume the Hobo Stance. This stance communicates a readiness to strike in defense if approached.

- **Thrust Push**: While in Single-Hand Sword Grip, Bicycle Grip, or Baseball Grip with the stick pointed toward the opponent, press the tip of the stick against the opponent's body, and apply firm pressure. To push him away, step forward using your body weight, simultaneously pushing the stick forward.

- **Enhanced Thrust Push**: In a similar fashion, while in Single-Hand Sword Grip, Bicycle Grip, or Baseball Grip With the stick pointed toward the opponent, press the tip of the stick against the opponent's body while placing the butt of your stick against your hip. Walk straight forward, continually pushing forward. Once you have the opponent on the move, Thrust the Walking Stick forward to make additional space.

- **Horizontal Push**: While in Bicycle or Rifle grip from ready position, use the Walking Stick to forcefully push the opponent back.

- **Figure-Eight Barrier**: While in any of the grips, rapidly perform a figure-eight motion facing the assailant so that they will be struck if they try to advance. This creates a dynamic barrier between you and the aggressor. It is a good way to keep an opponent at bay for a short time.

If the aggressor continues to press, transition to a flurry of strikes targeting the extremities first. A good strike to the hand will likely disable the aggressor sufficiently to have them retreat. If you need to close the distance to short-range, do so by striking as you close in. A good progression targets the hand (weapon hand if one is involved), followed by the arm and then the head.

Body and Shirt Grab Counters

If an assailant grabs you from behind, or grabs your clothing, there are a variety of ways to escape and counter one can use to efficiently break away and counter. Note that the methods shown in this section are a sampling of effective methods. Future editions of this document will expand the methodologies.

Bear Hug Counter

Turn and dip body sharply, thrusting tip of the stick into the opponent.

The crotch, bladder, and gut are all good targets.

Turning your body sharply generates the power of the delivered thrust.

Once you have broken free of the hold, perform a blitz of strikes.

Single Hand Shirt Grab Method 1

In the instance that the assailant grasps your right side shirt sleeve or collar, turn your body to the right bringing the butt of the cane up and to the outside of the opponent's arm. The mirror image of this method would be employed if the assailant grasps your left side shirt sleeve or collar.

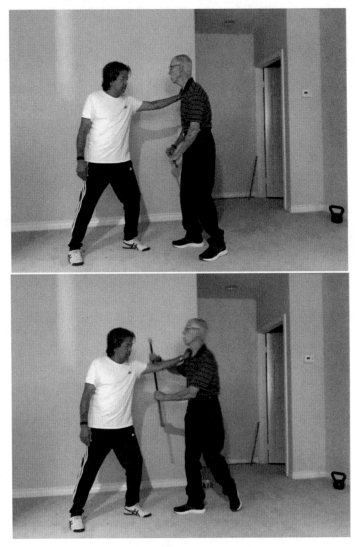

Step back with the left foot, bringing the stick's tip down and the butt of the Walking Cane up.

Perform a rowing motion, bringing the tip of the cane past your left hip.

Having broken free, begin to immediately execute a Blitz of strikes.

Single Hand Shirt Grab Method 2

Another method to disengage an assailant who is grasping your right side shirt sleeve or collar, is to employ the hooking method. The mirror image of this method would be employed if the assailant grasps your left side shirt sleeve or collar.

Turning your body to the left, simultaneously bringing the tip of the cane down to your left hip, and the ball end up and the opponent's arm.

Hook the butt end of the cane over the opponent's arm close to the wrist while simultaneously turning your body to the right, stepping forward with your left foot, and bringing the butt of the cane down close to the right hip with the tip end of the Walking Cane up.

Follow through using a rowing motion, turning the opponent around so that their back is exposed.

Having broken free, begin to execute a Blitz of strikes.

Continue striking until the threat is eliminated.

Single Hand Shirt Grab Method Standing Side to Side, Facing the Same Way

A method to disengage an assailant who is grasping your right-side shirt sleeve or collar while standing side to side facing the same way, can also employ using the hooking method. The mirror image of this method will be employed if the assailant grasps your left side shirt sleeve or collar.

Begin to turn your body to the right.

As you turn to the right, start to bring the butt of the cane up.

Turning swiftly to the right, bring the butt of the cane up, back, and outside of the assailant's left arm and the tip near your right hip.

Follow through performing a rowing motion, bringing the tip of the cane down past the right hip while simultaneously stepping back with the left foot.

Follow through performing a rowing motion, bringing the butt of the cane down past the right while simultaneously stepping back with the left foot.

Turn the opponent to potentially expose their back.

Having broken free, immediately execute a blitz of strikes.

Single Hand Shirt Grab From the Side Facing the Opposite Way

Another method to disengage an assailant grasping your right side shirt sleeve or collar employs the simple motion of breaking hard against the attacker's elbow. The mirror image of this method would be employed if the assailant grasps your left side shirt sleeve or collar.

If an assailant grabs your right sleeve or collar while standing side to side facing the opposite way, begin turning your body to the right.

Keep turning while targeting the back of the attacker's elbow.

Hit the back of the attacker's right elbow hard with the walking cane shaft disengaging their hold.

Having broken free, immediately execute a Blitz of strikes.

Double Hand Shirt Grab and Choke Counters

Note that the methods shown in this section are a sampling of effective methods. Future editions of this document will expand the methodologies.

Double Hand Shirt Grab Method 1

In the instance that the assailant grasps your shoulder level clothing with both hands, employ the figure eight concept to efficiently escape the hold. The same method may be used if faced with a frontal double hand choke.

Execute the first half of a figure eight by turning your body to the left, bringing the butt of the cane near your right hip and the tip up to the outside of the assailant's right arm to your left.

Perform a rowing motion, bringing the butt of the cane down past the right hip in a figure eight motion while simultaneously stepping back with the right foot.

Follow through with the rowing motion.

Continue the rowing motion so that the attacker's side or back is exposed to you.

Having broken free, immediately execute a Blitz of strikes.

Double Hand Shirt Grab Method 2

To disengage an assailant when they grab your shoulder-level clothing with both hands is to employ the figure eight concept to efficiently escape the hold. The same method may be used if faced with a frontal double-hand choke. Note: The mirror image of this method may be performed leading with the butt end of the cane.

Bring the tip of the cane straight up through the middle of the opponents' arms.

As a variant to this method, the tip of the cane can be used to strike up under the assailant's chin.

Once the cane is threaded through the attacker's arms, turn the cane counterclockwise with the tip of the cane over their right arm and the butt end under their left arm while simultaneously stepping back with the left foot.

Continue the counterclockwise rotation until broken free.

Having broken free, immediately execute a Blitz of strikes.

Double Hand Shirt Grab Method 3

Another way to disengage an assailant when they grasp your shoulder-level clothing with both hands is to employ the figure eight concept to efficiently escape the hold. The same method may be used if faced with a frontal double-hand choke.

Release the tip end of the cane (left hand).

Begin rotating the cane counterclockwise.

Fully rotate the cane so that is horizontal over the assailant's arms.

Grab tip end of the cane.

Bring Cane down sharply smashing into the assailant.

Having broken free, immediately execute a Blitz of strikes.

Countering Opponents Walking Cane Shaft Grabs

If the aggressor grabs any portion of the Walking Canes shaft, you must regain control quickly. Prior to implementing the counter, a sudden, very sharp push or pull jolting action, in any direction, will often temporarily stun the attacker. The Grab Counter should follow the jolting action immediately.

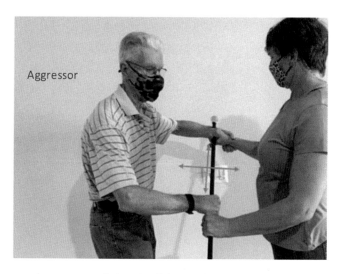

As soon as the aggressor has grasped the Walking Stick shaft, with one or both hands utilize a basic rowing motion depicted in the following series of images. Note that the method may be employed with a right or left lead.

Begin to rotate the left end of the Walking Cane up and the right end down. The motion is similar to paddling a canoe. Simultaneously if the Walking Stick is turning to the right and down, begin to step back with the right foot. Similarly, if the Walking Stick is turning to the left and down, begin to step back with the left foot.

Continued Motion

Continued Motion

Continued Motion

Pull the Right end of the Walking Cane sharply down past the right hip.

Having regained control of the walking cane, begin a blitz of strikes.

Continue striking until the threat is eliminated.

The common Walking Cane Grabs are presented in the following images.

Both assailant's hands grasp the Walking Cane outside of the defender's hands.

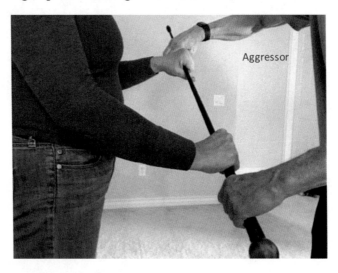

Both of aggressor's hands grasp the Walking Cane inside of defender's hands.

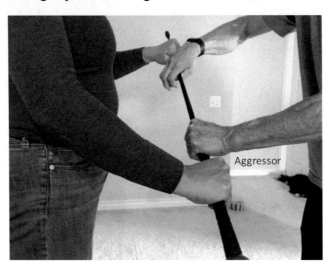

One of the Aggressor's hands is grasping the Walking Cane inside of the defender's hands, while the other hand grasps outside of the defender's hands.

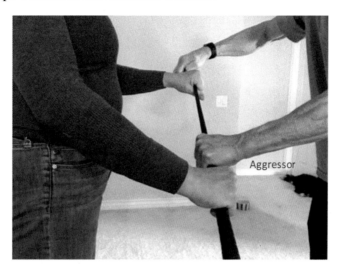

One of the Aggressor's hands grasps one of the defender's wrists, while the other hand grasps the Walking Cane shaft inside or outside the defender's hands.

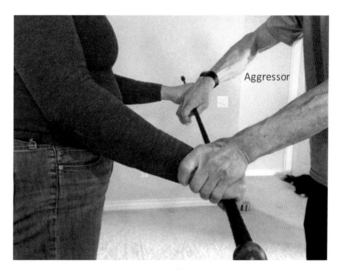

Both of the assailant's hands are grasping both of the wrists of the defender.

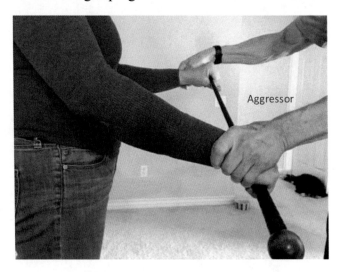

Walking Cane Tip End Grab Counter

If the attacker grabs the tip end of the Walking Cane, you must regain control quickly. Prior to implementing the following methods, a sudden, very sharp push or pull jolting action will often temporarily stun the attacker. The Grab Counter should follow the jolting action immediately.

- Method 1: Push Pull:

  If the Opponent Grabs the tip end of the Walking Cane, switch to Bicycle or Rifle Grip immediately. With the end of the Walking Stick pointed directly at the opponent, Push and pull the Walking Cane forward and back sharply and repeatedly. Add a step back or forward if the cane is not freed quickly. The addition of the step to the rear will enhance the force of the pull. Once the Cane is free immediately execute a blitz of strikes.

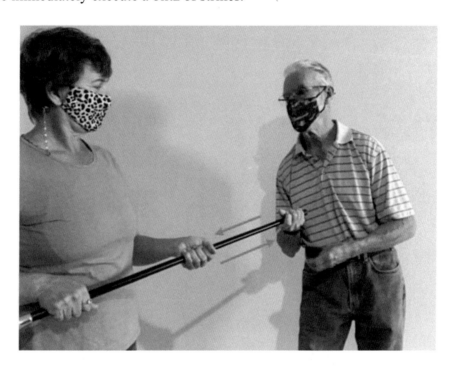

- Method 2: Tip Rotation:

If the opponent grabs the tip end of the Walking Cane, switch to Bicycle or Rifle Grip immediately. With the end of the Walking Cane pointed at the opponent, rotate the tip of the walking stick clockwise or counterclockwise. If the rotation is met with resistance, switch the rotation direction. Note that stepping back while rotating the tip of the Walking Stick can aid in freeing the tip. Additionally, placing the ball end of the stick in the hollow of your hip provides a good mechanical base when rotating the tip of the Walking Stick. Once the stick is free, immediately execute a blitz of strikes. Both methods 1 and 2 may be combined in any order to break free of the opponent's grasp. Beginning the technique with a feint, sudden push/pull, or by starting with a rotation reversal momentarily often shocks the opponent facilitating a quick hold break.

Begin by rotating the tip of the walking stick (Clockwise or Counterclockwise).

If resistance is met, change the direction of rotation.

When the tip of the Walking Cane has broken free, execute a blitz of strikes. While either Method 1 or 2 are effective, using a combination of both methods can enhance effectiveness.

Keeping the Knob end at Distance

While the Tip End Grab counters can also work for the Butt or Ball end of the walking cane, it can be much more difficult to do so as the shape and size of the butt end gives the opponent grip advantage. It is best to keep the butt end at a distance when possible. As you can discern from the images below, the larger the Butt or Ball end of the walking cane gives the attacker more control making it difficult to escape.

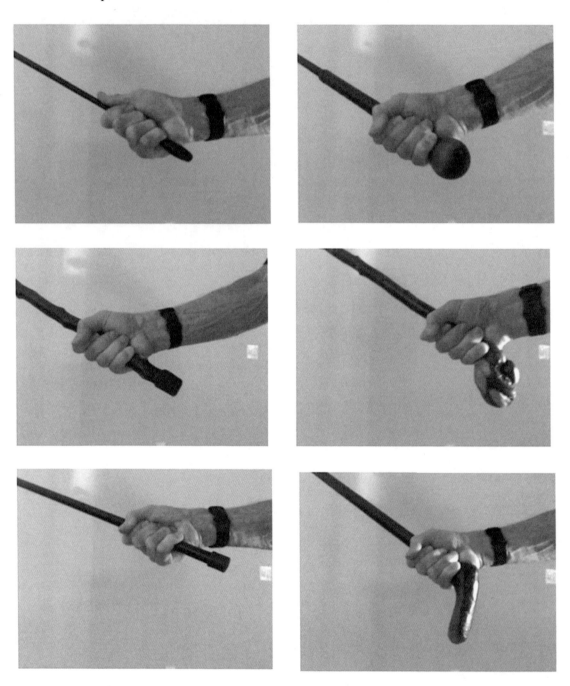

Role Playing Exercises

Awareness and Defensive Posturing Exercise (Role Playing)

Sidewalk Walking: If you encounter a person that you consider a threat, or hear someone walking toward you, or approaching from behind; turn perpendicular toward the direction of travel and assume the Horizontal at Ease Stance.

- Horizontal at Ease Stance: Walking Stick is in either the Bicycle or Rifle Grip. This is the recommended non-threatening ready stance.

From this position, if necessary, you can easily perform strikes 6, 7, 8, and 9 quickly and efficiently. Strikes 8 and 9 are very quick and efficient lower-body strikes. They can quickly stifle the aggressor's advance. Follow up with a series of strikes to end the confrontation.

Begin with a partner walking down a sidewalk with the partner playing the role of aggressor walking up behind you (or simulate a sidewalk in an open area). Using your Street Smart skills, determine that you may be followed by someone with bad intent. Turn ninety degrees with the intention of letting the person pass. If he says a pleasant day and passes, your Spidey senses were likely not correct this time. If they reach to grab or advance in a threatening manner, you are perfectly stationed to defend yourself. Keep in mind that you should use as much discretion as possible. Whoever touches first is, by law, the person who initiated an assault. If you hit first, you should be very certain their intention is to harm you. Repeat the exercise with the aggressor approaching from the front.

Potential assailant is approaching from behind. Detect the approach and move over into the non-threatening position.

If the threat is real, execute a block or strike immediately. Follow up with a blitz of strikes.

Engagement Exercises (Role Playing)

Scenario 1: Begin with the student in the Horizontal at Ease Stance: Walking Stick is in either the Bicycle or Rifle Grip. As the aggressor approaches, the student assumes a keep-away technique (such as thrust push or horizontal push). This exercise should be expanded upon to simulate varying encounter scenarios.

Scenario 2: Begin with the student in the Horizontal at Ease Stance: Walking Stick is in either the Bicycle or Rifle Grip. As the aggressor approaches, the student changes to the one-hand Sword grip. Initially, employ the figure 8 pattern to keep the aggressor at Long-Range. Follow on with a simulated Long-Range blitz (series of strikes). Execute a series of Long-Range strikes (at least 3 strikes). This exercise should be expanded upon to simulate varying encounter scenarios.

Scenario 3: It is important to stress the usefulness of training close-quarter engagement with the student. The first reaction of untrained individuals will usually be to try to keep an engagement at long-range. Aggressors will likely try to close the distance to inflict harm or subdue an individual as an opening move. Having a level of comfort in close quarters will enhance the ability to protect oneself. Begin with the student in the Horizontal at Ease Stance. Walking Stick is in either the Bicycle or Rifle Grip. In this scenario, the aggressor closes the distance quickly. The student uses the Walking stick to engage the aggressor using parries, redirects, and strikes while in the Bicycle or Rifle Grip. Practice employing the figure 8 concept of blitzing the opponent with multiple strikes. Employ the concept of redirects, blocks, and strikes as part of the whole encounter. This exercise should be expanded upon to simulate varying scenarios, including Horizontal Pushes, Horizontal Slams, and transition from short to long and long to short-range.

Scenario 4: Begin with the student in the Horizontal at Ease Stance: Walking Stick is in either the Bicycle or Rifle Grip. In this scenario, the aggressor closes the distance quickly. The student uses the Walking stick to engage the aggressor using strikes while in the Bicycle or Rifle Grip. Insert at any point stick grabs to practice Countering Stick Grab techniques. This exercise should be expanded upon to include varying stick grabs.

Obviously, there are many situations that could be simulated. Given any real data on actual events in your area, develop training scenarios that may help in those instances.

Turning and Pivoting Exercises

As an example, the need to be able to turn about abruptly presents the scenario of an off leashed dog charging from an unspecified direction.

With the student facing the 12:00 position, call out a variety of clock numbers having the student Pivot so that they are facing that direction. Once at the new position, have them reset to the original 12:00 direction prior to calling out a new direction. Start slowly using only the 12, 3, 6, and 9 positions. As the student becomes more confident, have them execute the exercise using all directions relative to the clock face. As a further challenge, have the student execute the exercise from their current orientation without resetting to the 12:00 position.

Walking Stick Warmup/Affinity Exercises

Performing simple warmup exercises regularly helps the student maintain familiarity with the Walking Stick as a Self Defense tool. The exercises develop fluidity with striking combinations and dynamic grip changes. Being able to change grips on the fly allows the student to alternate between long and short-range seamlessly. Encourage the student to practice the exercises at least twice a week for 10 to 20 minutes. This will help to maintain a basic skill set.

Basic Warm-Up Exercise #1

Starting from Ready Bicycle Grip

- o Execute strikes 2 & 3 in a figure 8 pattern for a number of reps.
- o Follow up executing strikes 4 & 5 in figure 8 for a number of reps.
- o Repeat the pattern for the Sword Grip, Baseball Grip, and Rifle Grip.

Basic Warm-Up Exercise #2

Starting from Ready Bicycle Grip

- o Transition to Sword grip and immediately execute strikes 2 & 3 in a figure 8 pattern twice.
- o Transition to Baseball Grip and immediately execute strikes 2 & 3 in a figure 8 pattern twice.

- o Transition to Rifle Grip and immediately execute strikes 2 & 3 in a figure 8 pattern twice.

- o Transition to Bicycle Grip and immediately execute strikes 2 & 3 in a figure 8 pattern twice.

- o Repeat the pattern several times.

Basic Warm-Up Exercise #3

Starting from Ready Bicycle Grip

- o Transition to Sword grip and immediately execute strikes 4 & 5 in a figure 8 pattern twice.

- o Transition to Baseball Grip and immediately execute strikes 4 & 5 in a figure 8 pattern twice.

- o Transition to Rifle Grip and immediately execute strikes 4 & 5 in a figure 8 pattern twice.

- o Transition to Bicycle Grip and immediately execute strikes 4 & 5 in a figure 8 pattern twice.

- o Repeat the pattern several times.

Forms (Katas)

Practicing simple exercises (forms) is an excellent way for the student to become comfortable handling the walking stick for defensive purposes. Performed regularly, they reinforce the person's skills with the Walking Stick. They are also valuable for seniors and individuals with balance and coordination issues.

Form #1

(Beginning: Single-Hand Sword Grip, Right Hand) (Intermediate: Each Grip independent)

Initial Position is with the right hand on top of the stick, in a normal stance.

Slide your hand forward and down to single-hand grip.

- o Step forward with the right foot and execute Strike #1.

- o Step forward with the left foot and execute Strike #2.

- o Step forward with the right foot and execute Strike #3.

Turn:

- o Step forward with the left foot and execute Strike #4.

- o Step forward with the right foot and execute Strike #5.

- o Step forward with the left foot and execute Strike #6.

Turn:

- o   Step forward with the right foot and execute Strike #7.

- o   Step back with the right foot and execute Strike #8.

- o   Step forward with the right foot and execute Strike #9.

Turn:

- o   Step forward with the right foot and execute Strike #10.

- o   Step back with the right foot and execute Strike #11.

- o   Step forward with the right foot and execute Strike #12.

Form #2

(Changing Grips, Right Hand) (Balance Intensive)

Initial Position is Bicycle Grip, in a normal stance.

This form is for the student who wishes to challenge themselves with a neuromuscular exercise to enhance their balance and coordination while keeping sharp on striking techniques.

Assume Single-Handed Sword Grip.

- o   Step forward with the right foot and execute Strike #1.

- o   Step forward with the left foot and execute Strike #2.

- o   Step forward with the right foot and execute Strike #3.

Switch to Bicycle Grip.

Turn:

- o   Step forward with the left foot and execute Strike #4.

- o   Step forward with the right foot and execute Strike #5.

- o   Step forward with the left foot and execute Strike #6.

Switch to Baseball Grip.

Turn:

- o   Step forward with the right foot and execute Strike #7.

- o   Step forward with the left foot and execute Strike #8.

- o   Step forward with the right foot and execute Strike #9.

Switch to Rifle Grip.

Turn:

- Step forward with the left foot and execute Strike #10.
- Step forward with the right foot and execute Strike #11.
- Step forward with the left foot and execute Strike #12.

The form may be executed left-handed, changing the strike pattern to the left-hand pattern.

Form #3

Start from the ready position (Left foot forward Bicycle Grip).

1) Step forward with the right foot and **execute strike 1** with the **Butt** of the Walking Cane.

2) Step forward with the left foot and **execute strike 2** with the **Tip** of the Walking Cane.

3) Hook Stance right turn and clear.

4) Step forward with the right foot and **execute strike 3** with the **Butt** of the Walking Cane.

5) Step back with the right foot and **execute strike 4** with the **Tip** of the Walking Cane.

6) Step forward with the right foot and **execute strike 5** with the **Butt** of the Walking Cane.

7) Step forward with the left foot and execute strike 6 with the **Tip** of the Walking Cane.

8) Hook stance right turn and clear.

9) Step forward with the right foot and **execute strike 7** with the **Butt** of the Walking Cane.

10) Step back with the right foot and **execute strike 8** with the **Tip** of the Walking Cane.

11) Step forward with the right foot and **execute strike 9** with the **Butt** of the Walking Cane.

12) Step forward with the left foot and **execute strike 10** with the **Butt** of the Walking Cane.

13) Hook stance right turn and clear.

14) Step forward with the right foot and **execute strike 11** with the **Tip** of the Walking Cane.

15) Step back with the right foot and **execute strike 12** with the **Tip** of the Walking Cane.

16) Step forward with the right foot and **execute strike 1** with the **Butt** of the Walking Cane.

17) Step forward with the left foot and **execute strike 2** with the **Tip** of the Walking Cane.

18) Hook stance right turn and clear.

19) Step forward with the right foot and **execute strike 3** with the **Butt** of the Walking Cane.

20) Step back with the right foot and **execute strike 4** with the **Tip** of the Walking Cane.

21) Step forward with the right foot and **execute strike** 5 with the **Butt** of the Walking Cane.

22) Step forward with the left foot and **execute strike 6** with the **Tip** of the Walking Cane.

23) Hook stance right turn and clear.

24) Step forward with the right foot and **execute strike 7** with the **Butt** of the Walking Cane.

25) Step back with the right foot and **execute strike** with the **Tip** of the Walking Cane.

26) Step forward with the right foot and **execute strike 9** with the **Butt** of the Walking Cane.

27) Step forward with the left foot and **execute strike 10** with the **Butt** of the Walking Cane.

28) Hook stance right turn and clear.

29) Step forward with the right foot and **execute strike 11** with the **Tip** of the Walking Cane.

30) Step back **even** with the right foot and **execute strike 12** with the **Tip** of the Walking Cane.

Walking Stick Techniques for Mobility Assistance

The Walking Stick, also known as the Walking Cane, is a practical tool for use as an assistive mobility device. Learning how to use the cane properly is essential to maintaining balance while walking and preventing falls. Prior to using the Walking Cane as an Assistive Mobility Device, you should <u>always</u> consult your Doctor or Physical Therapist to ensure that your individual physical issues are addressed. You may require a cane for a short period of time following an injury or accident, or it may be your constant companion if you suffer from a chronic debilitating disease. Either way, determining the correct height of the walking cane is crucial because it leads to appropriate balance and stability, generating greater confidence and safety (*see Appendix G:* Determining Walking Stick Height for Mobility Assistance). Note that the internet is a great source of information on proper cane use.

Use of a cane may be recommended for many conditions including:

- Leg fractures

- Severe knee or hip arthritis

- Knee or hip surgery

- Stroke rehabilitation

- Frailty due to old age, inactivity, or illness

- Degenerative movement disorders include Parkinson's disease, Multiple sclerosis, and Huntington's disease.

When using the cane for gait issues due to an injured or affected leg:

- Hold the cane in the hand on your "good" side so that it provides support to the opposite leg.

- Take a step with the "bad" leg and bring the cane forward at the same time, moving the cane and affected leg forward together.

- Plant the cane firmly on the ground before stepping forward with the stronger leg.

- Lean your weight through the arm holding the cane as needed.

- Always have the bad leg assume the first full weight-bearing step on level surfaces.

- The cane should be moved the distance of one average step forward with each step.

Walking up and down stairs with a cane can be challenging.

When using a cane on stairs, it is important to always be as safe as possible and use the railing if the stairs have one. Place your entire foot on the next step and apply force through the heel. You should always lead with your strongest or good leg. This is especially true when using a cane on the stairs. To help you remember this, think about this saying: "up is good, down in bad."

- To go up stairs using a cane, hold onto the handrail, put your stronger leg on the first stair step, and shift your body weight to step up with both the affected (weaker) leg and the cane at the same time until they meet with your strong leg on the first stair step. Always face forward. You're much less stable when you're turned sideways, especially if the staircase has no handrail. Repeat this process while climbing up the stairs until you reach the top of the staircase.

- To go down stairs with a cane, hold onto the handrail; put your weight on your stronger (unaffected) leg, move the cane down to the next step below you, and then move the weaker leg down to the step the cane is now balancing on. Always face forward. You're much less stable when you're turned sideways, especially if the staircase has no handrail. Repeat this process while climbing down the stairs until you reach the bottom landing of the stairs.

The Walking Stick may also be used as a mobility tool to perform everyday actions. Many seniors have trouble standing up when sitting on a chair or couch (a deep couch can impede anyone). As previously stated, prior to using the Walking Stick as an Assistive Mobility Device, you should always consult your Doctor or Physical Therapist to ensure that your individual physical issues are addressed. The methods shown here are only one way to utilize the Walking Stick/Cane. Depending on the individual's fitness level, other methods may be recommended by your Doctor or Physical Therapist.

Standing up using the couch/chair armrest and Walking Stick for support starts with leaning forward and placing hands as depicted on the Walking Stick and armrest. To start, place the tip of the Walking Stick in line with your heels (Note: Ensure the tip of the Walking Stick is on a non-slip surface). Scoot forward using the armrest and Walking Stick to assist the forward motion to the front of the couch/chair.

Using cane and armrest for support and additional power, lean forward and push yourself up to a standing position.

Position the Walking Stick past the toes of your feet to ensure a good balanced position.

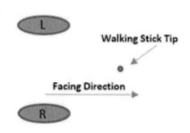

Standing up using the Walking Stick only for support starts with leaning forward and placing hands as depicted on the Walking Stick. To start, place the tip of the Walking Stick in line with your heels (Note: Ensure the tip of the Walking Stick is on a non-slip surface). Scoot forward using the Walking Stick to assist the forward motion to the front of the couch/chair.

Power up using the walking stick to assist. Position the Walking Stick past the toes of your feet to ensure a good balanced position.

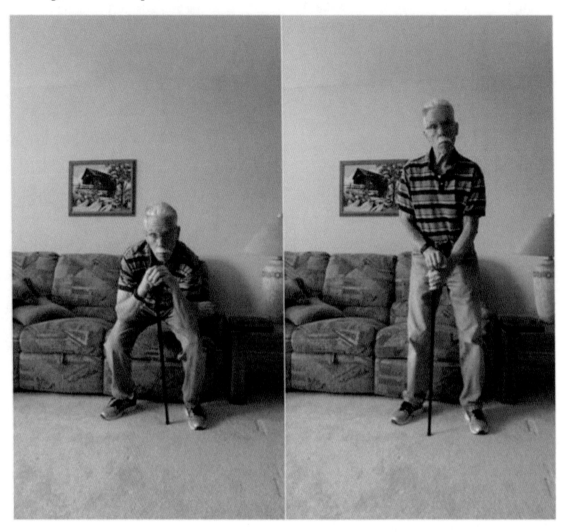

Getting up from sitting on the floor with Walking stick assistance starts with assuming a position with legs straight out.

Plant the tip of the Walking stick next to the left side in a rowing-the-boat position (depending on mobility issues, the mirror of this exercise may be utilized).

Bring the foot on the right side back, so that the knee is up.

Using the Walking Stick to power through sweep the left leg assist, begin to sweep the left leg under the right.

Complete the sweep with the left knee down.

Grasping the walking Stick with both hands, power up with the right leg and the Walking Stick.

Position the Walking Stick past the toes of your feet to ensure a good balanced position.

Getting up from lying on the floor face up. (Note: if you have fallen and find yourself on the floor, seek help immediately to assess any injuries that may have occurred prior to attempting to get up). Plant the Walking stick to the left side (depending on mobility issues, the mirror of this exercise may be utilized). Walking stick assistance starts with assuming a position with legs straight out.

Bring the left knee toward your chest and begin a roll to your right side using the Walking Stick to assist.

Plant the Walking Stick tip on the right as shown.

Keep the left hand gripped to the walking stick and position the right hand on the ground.

Sweep the right leg back through as shown.

Bring the trunk up to the kneeling position and power up to standing.

Position the Walking Stick past the toes of your feet to ensure a good balanced position.

Getting up from lying on the floor face down. (Note: if you have fallen and find yourself on the floor, seek help immediately to assess any injuries that may have occurred prior to attempting to get up). Plant the Walking stick to the left side (depending on mobility issues, the mirror of this exercise may be utilized). Walking stick assistance starts with assuming a position with legs straight out. Begin to move your upper body up using the Walking Stick to assist.

Using your hands to climb up the Walking Stick, begin to roll up into a side position.

While rolling up, move the left knee under the right leg.

Begin to bring the left leg up towards your chest using the Walking Stick for support and power.

Bring the left leg and then the right leg together so that you are in a kneeling position, using the Walking Stick for support.

Climb up the walking Stick, hand over hand, while beginning to bring the left foot forward.

With the left foot forward, power up to a standing position using the Walking Stick to assist power and stability.

Position the Walking Stick past the toes of your feet to ensure a good balanced position.

Getting up from bed can be difficult for people with mobility issues. Using the Walking Stick to assist begins by pushing yourself to a favorable position, so that you can start to get your legs over the side of the bed.

With one leg over the edge, place the Walking Stick on the floor. Begin pushing down while starting to move the left leg over the side of the bed.

With Both legs over the edge, begin pushing up to a sitting position using the Walking stick as support and additional power.

Once in a sitting position, take a moment to ensure you are steady enough to begin standing.

Once you feel stable, then position the Walking Stick directly in front of yourself in preparation to begin standing.

Begin to power up using the walking stick to assist by pushing down on it.

Continue to power up using the walking stick to assist by pushing down.

Position the Walking Stick past the toes of your feet to ensure a good balanced position.

Appendix A: Crime Report Information Sources

Sources for Crime Reports Maps and Information

Search the Web for:

- Crime Reports

- Crime Maps

- Local Crime news

- Local City News Paper

Simply search City Name Crime Reports

Examples for Los Angeles, California:

Local Newspaper: Local City News Paper: http://maps.latimes.com/crime/

LAPD

- o LAPD Crime Mapping

    - Get up-to-date crime statistics for neighborhoods throughout Los Angeles. Being informed about crime in your community is the first step in preventing future occurrences.

http://www.lapdonline.org/crime_mapping_and_compstat

Appendix B: Body Language

What Is Body Language?

Even when they don't verbally express their thoughts, most people constantly throw off clues to what they think and feel. Non-verbal messages communicated through the sender's body movements, facial expressions, vocal tone and volume, and other clues are collectively known as body language.

Body language isn't always as clear as a spoken language by far. How it is interpreted can play a big role in how someone relates to and interacts with others. These brief displays of emotion that an individual may try to conceal register in our brain almost immediately—even when we are not consciously aware of them.

Victim Selection and What to Do About It
Victim Selection And What to Do About It - Toughen Up

How to Read and Decode Body Language to Spot a Predator
https://www.healthline.com/health/body-language
https://www.forensicscolleges.com/blog/resources/forensic-psychologists-guide-to-body-language

Short Circuiting the Victim Selection Process
The Seven-Second Rule: How to Avoid Being an Easy Target (nbcnews.com)
7 Ways to Spot a Predator – Quick and Dirty Tips

Also see the book: *The Gift of Fear* by Gavin de Becker

Appendix C: Air Travel and TSA Information

TSA Cane Aircraft Carry on Confirmation: Facebook Messenger

Question sent to TSA with a photo of my Walking Cane:

Hello,
I am resending this message as I have not yet received a reply. My wife and I are planning a trip to see our daughter and grandchild. I use a cane to assist me keeping balance as I have Parkinson's disease. I looked on the American Airlines site which indicated that I can take my cane on board with me as part of my carryon. At my wife's insistence, I am double checking with you at TSA to assure that I can travel with my cane on the aircraft. My cane is 36 inches long. I have included a picture. I appreciate your assistance.
Thank You Len

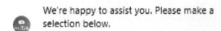

We're happy to assist you. Please make a selection below.

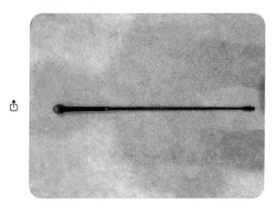

Reply from TSA:

Thanks for your message, a Social Care Specialist will be in touch shortly.

AskTSA Team members are on duty M-F (8:00 am – 10:00 pm eastern time) and Saturday, Sunday and holidays (9:00 am – 7:00 pm eastern time)

Thank you for reaching out to us, Len. Canes are allowed through the checkpoint. Please place it on the conveyor belt for X-ray screening. If you need to be immediately reunited with your cane after it has been screened by X-ray, please let our officer know. For more information on mobility aids, please visit: bit.ly/1OK638h
Safe travels. -Dom

We hope Ask TSA was able to answer your question, please provide your feedback by selecting a response to the survey below.

Open Survey

Canes may be brought on aircraft as carry-on or checked in.

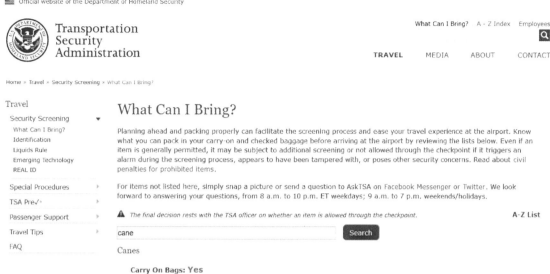

https://www.tsa.gov/travel/security-screening/whatcanibring/items/canes

https://www.tsa.gov/travel/security-screening/whatcanibring/items/ski-poles

Transportation
Security
Administration

What Can I Bring?   A - Z Index   Employees

TRAVEL   MEDIA   ABOUT   CONTACT

Home » Ski Poles

Travel

Security Screening   ▼
  What Can I Bring?
  Identification
  Liquids Rule
  Emerging Technology
  REAL ID

Special Procedures   ▶

TSA Pre✓®   ▶

Passenger Support   ▶

Travel Tips   ▶

FAQ

Ski Poles

Carry On Bags: No

Checked Bags: Yes

For more prohibited items, please go to the 'What Can I Bring?' page.

⚠ *The final decision rests with the TSA officer on whether an item is allowed through the checkpoint.*

https://www.tsa.gov/travel/security-screening/whatcanibring/items/hiking-poles

Transportation
Security
Administration

What Can I Bring?   A - Z Index   Employees

TRAVEL   MEDIA   ABOUT   CONTACT

Home » Hiking Poles

Travel

Security Screening   ▼
  What Can I Bring?
  Identification
  Liquids Rule
  Emerging Technology
  REAL ID

Special Procedures   ▶

TSA Pre✓®   ▶

Passenger Support   ▶

Travel Tips   ▶

FAQ

Hiking Poles

Carry On Bags: No

Checked Bags: Yes

For more prohibited items, please go to the 'What Can I Bring?' page.

⚠ *The final decision rests with the TSA officer on whether an item is allowed through the checkpoint.*

Airline Mobility Device Information

Plan Travel   Travel Information   AAdvantage

🏠 Home › Special assistance › Mobility and medical devices

Mobility and medical devices

Traveling with mobility and medical devices

If you're traveling with any medical device, a wheelchair or other mobility device we're here to help – we offer pre-boarding, deplaning and airport assistance

For battery operated mobility devices, contact Special Assistance to make sure the battery type is approved for travel and for any other special assistance travel requests

Contact Special Assistance »

If you're connecting to another airline or traveling on a codeshare flight, contact the operating carrier or other airline for their rules on traveling with mobility and medical devices

⊙ Tips and suggestions

Carry-on devices

Mobility and medical devices don't count toward carry-on limits. If space is limited, the device doesn't fit in the cabin or if it isn't required during the flight, it may need to be checked. These include

- Canes, walkers, continuous positive airway pressure machines (CPAP) and other assistive devices that can be collapsed to fit into overhead and under-seat storage
- Items used for comfort such as seat cushions, arm or footrests

https://www.aa.com/i18n/travel-info/special-assistance/mobility-and-medical-devices.jsp

Appendix D: Cane Handles

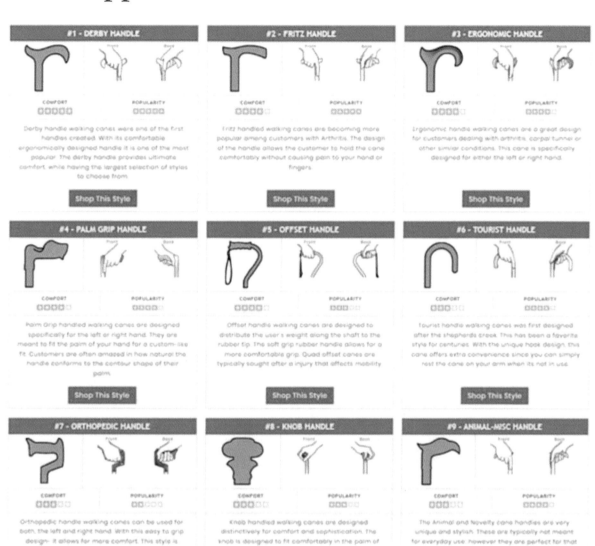

#1 - DERBY HANDLE
COMFORT ☐☐☐☐☐ POPULARITY ☐☐☐☐☐

Derby handle walking canes were one of the first handles created. With its comfortable ergonomically designed handle it is one of the most popular. The derby handle provides ultimate comfort, while having the largest selection of styles to choose from.

Shop This Style

#2 - FRITZ HANDLE
COMFORT ☐☐☐☐ POPULARITY ☐☐☐☐☐

Fritz handled walking canes are becoming more popular among customers with Arthritis. The design of the handle allows the customer to hold the cane comfortably without causing pain to your hand or fingers.

Shop This Style

#3 - ERGONOMIC HANDLE
COMFORT ☐☐☐☐ POPULARITY ☐☐☐☐

Ergonomic handle walking canes are a great design for customers dealing with arthritis, carpal tunnel or other similar conditions. This cane is specifically designed for either the left or right hand.

Shop This Style

#4 - PALM GRIP HANDLE
COMFORT ☐☐☐☐ POPULARITY ☐☐☐☐

Palm Grip handled walking canes are designed specifically for the left or right hand. They are meant to fit the palm of your hand for a custom-like fit. Customers are often amazed in how natural the handle conforms to the contour shape of their palm.

Shop This Style

#5 - OFFSET HANDLE
COMFORT ☐☐☐☐ POPULARITY ☐☐☐☐

Offset handle walking canes are designed to distribute the user's weight along the shaft to the rubber tip. The soft grip rubber handle allows for a more comfortable grip. Quad offset canes are typically sought after a injury that affects mobility.

Shop This Style

#6 - TOURIST HANDLE
COMFORT ☐☐☐☐ POPULARITY ☐☐☐☐

Tourist handle walking canes was first designed after the shepherds crook. This has been a favorite style for centuries. With the unique hook design, this cane offers extra convenience since you can simply rest the cane on your arm when its not in use.

Shop This Style

#7 - ORTHOPEDIC HANDLE
COMFORT ☐☐☐☐ POPULARITY ☐☐☐☐

Orthopedic handle walking canes can be used for both, the left and right hand. With this easy to grip design- it allows for more comfort. This style is typically one that your Doctor would recommend.

#8 - KNOB HANDLE
COMFORT ☐☐☐☐ POPULARITY ☐☐☐☐

Knob handled walking canes are designed distinctively for comfort and sophistication. The knob is designed to fit comfortably in the palm of your hand.

#9 - ANIMAL-MISC HANDLE
COMFORT ☐☐☐☐ POPULARITY ☐☐☐☐

The Animal and Novelty cane handles are very unique and stylish. These are typically not meant for everyday use; however they are perfect for that special event or occasion.

Appendix E: Walking Stick (AKA Walking Cane) Online Sources

The Black Swift **Walking Stick is an excellent choice. It is light, super strong, durable and fast. Cutting off the top of a rubber golf club grip that will tightly slip onto the Black Swift will provide excellent non-slip grip. I used hair gel as a lubricant in order to get the golf grip all the way up to the base of the handle. It also acts as an adhesive as it dries**
http://www.blackswiftsticks.com/

Cold Steel is another source for walking Sticks with a wide selection. The Cold Steel City Stick Walking Stick is a heavier Walking Stick. Extremely durable, strong, and fashionable.
Search on site: https://www.coldsteel.com

Brazos Walking Sticks
https://www.brazos-walking-sticks.com

Fashionable Canes: Blackthorn Shillelagh Fighting Stick Cane - Full Size Replica
https://www.fashionablecanes.com/blackthorn-shillelagh-fighting-stick-cane-full-size-replica.html?list=Category%20Listing%20-%20Irish%20Blackthorn%20Walking%20Sticks

Unbreakable Umbrella
The umbrella may be a good option for some due to the climate. A truly strong model can be found at: https://unbreakableumbrella.com/

McCaffrey Irish Store Blackthorn Walking Stick
https://mccaffreycrafts.com/

If you search the web for walking stick or walking cane, additional sites will be available to you to find the best model for your use.

Appendix F: Determining Walking Stick Height for Mobility Assistance

A walking stick/cane may be either a temporary or permanent solution. You may need a cane for a short period of time following an injury or accident, or it may be your constant companion if you suffer from a chronic debilitating disease. Either way, determining the correct height of the walking cane is important as it leads to appropriate balance and stability, which allows you greater confidence (and safety) in mobility.

To find the proper Height for the cane:

- Have the individual stand up straight in their normal walking shoes with their arms hanging naturally at their sides.

- Measure the distance from the floor to the wrist joint, rounding to the nearest half-inch.

- If the primary use will be for balance, adding an extra one to two inches to the height may be appropriate.

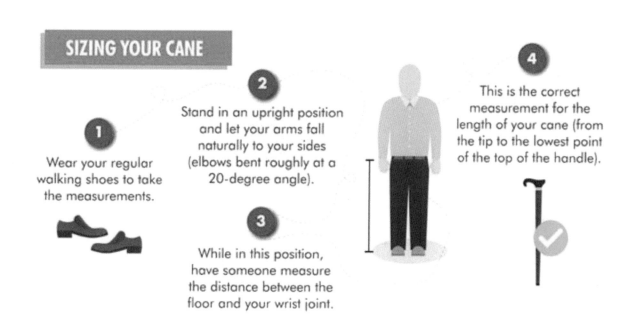

SIZING YOUR CANE

1 Wear your regular walking shoes to take the measurements.

2 Stand in an upright position and let your arms fall naturally to your sides (elbows bent roughly at a 20-degree angle).

3 While in this position, have someone measure the distance between the floor and your wrist joint.

4 This is the correct measurement for the length of your cane (from the tip to the lowest point of the top of the handle).

Appendix G: Proper Cane Use Information Links

"A Detailed Guide on How to Use a Cane for Balance Problem"
A Definitive Guide: How to Use A Cane for Balance Problem (seniorspride.com)

"How To Walk with a Cane Properly (For Walking With STABILITY)"
How To Use a Cane Properly (For Walking With STABILITY) (mobilitydeck.com)

Appendix H: Self Defense Law

Self-Defense Law: Overview - FindLaw

Link to Free Book covering Self Defense Law Principals
The Law of SELF Defense Principles
By Attorney Andrew F. Branca
Free Book Deal – Law of Self Defense

   To search for Self-Defense laws for your region/State Search format (STATE Self-Defense Law). The search will lead to a variety of links that cover the various elements and definitions of the state's law.

   For example searching Minnesota Self-Defense Law Penal Code yields the following with links to elements and definitions of the law.

   This search yields:

   o Minnesota's self-defense laws are codified in Minnesota Statues §609.06. In Minnesota, a person acts in self-defense when they reasonably believe force is necessary and uses only the level of force reasonably necessary to prevent the bodily harm feared. The intentional taking of the life of another is not authorized by section 609.06, except when necessary in resisting or preventing an offense which the actor reasonably believes exposes the actor or another to great bodily harm or dealth, or preventing the commission of a felony in the actor's place of abode.

   Another example searching: Oregon Self Defense Law penal code

   This search yields the information and links from various law firms specializing in self defense law for Oregon.